THE STORY

THIRTY-SECOND REGIMENT

MASSACHUSETTS INFANTRY.

WHENCE IT CAME; WHERE IT WENT; WHAT IT SAW;
AND WHAT IT DID.

By FRANCIS J. PARKER, COLONEL.

BOSTON:
C. W. CALKINS & CO., PUBLISHERS.
1880.

TO THE OFFICERS AND SOLDIERS

OF THE

THIRTY-SECOND MASSACHUSETTS,

IN MEMORY OF THE DEAD

AND

IN HONOR OF THE LIVING.

ERRATUM.

On page 3, twelfth line, for " Brevet Brigadier-General," read " Colonel." Colonel Prescott was never breveted.

PREFACE.

THIS book is not a history of the civil war, nor even
of the Army of the Potomac; but merely the story of one
of the regiments which composed that Army. It does not
relate the biography of the many distinguished generals
under whose command the battalion served, and the
endeavor has been made to exclude from it not only discussions as to the merits of individuals, but even favorable
or unfavorable opinions, save when the facts related
implied or seemed to require such reflections.

The book is intended chiefly to collect and present in
narrative form, descriptions of some of the experiences of
our Regiment, in order to preserve them in the memory of
those who were actors in the scenes described, and enable
the officers and men of the 32d to place in the hands of
their children and friends vivid pictures of the dangers,
trials, and pleasures which attended the service of our
soldiers in the war for the Union.

In the preparation of the book, I have received, and
gratefully acknowledge, the assistance of many of my old
comrades, officers, and men, not only by way of incidents
related verbally, but also — and this especially concerning
events which occurred after my own resignation — by way
of written contributions. Many of these are embodied in
the text almost in the language of the writers, and others
in a more or less condensed form. Among those to whom
I am thus indebted should be particularly named General

Luther Stephenson, jr., Surgeon Z. B. Adams, Major E. S. Farnsworth, General J. A. Cunningham, Sergeant S. C. Spaulding, Major Ambrose Bancroft, Captains G. W. Lauriat and J. C. Fuller; and last, but by no means least, Surgeon W. L. Faxon and Mrs. Faxon, whose memories have provided stores of incident. To Colonel I. F. Kingsbury I am indebted for the result of time-consuming researches in the Adjutant-General's Department of the State.

While making these just acknowledgments I absolve all those named from any responsibility for such literary imperfections as may appear herein and, assuming to myself all blame for such defects, must ask my readers to consider in charity to me the difficulties which must attend a work so composed, and at the last somewhat hastily completed.

F. J. P.

Boston, April 30th, 1880.

CONTENTS.

PREFACE vii

I.

IN GARRISON 1

II.

ON OUR OWN HOOK 28

III.

ON THE PENINSULA 43

IV.

CAMPAIGNING UNDER POPE 64

V.

OUR THIRD BATTALION 75

(ix.)

x. CONTENTS.

VI.

THE ANTIETAM CAMPAIGN 85

VII.

AFTER ANTIETAM . , ... 107

VIII.

TO FREDERICKSBURG 117

IX.

BETWEEN CAMPAIGNS 136

X.

CHANCELLORSVILLE 150

XI.

FREDERICKSBURG TO GETTYSBURG 159

XII.

AFTER GETTYSBURG 175

XIII.

A LADY AT WINTER QUARTERS 183

XIV.

AT LIBERTY 189

XV.

Out on Picket 196

XVI.

On Furlough 204

XVII.

The Wilderness Campaign 208

XVIII.

The Bomb Proofs 223

XIX.

Our Corps Hospital 228

XX.

About Petersburg 234

XXI.

The Last Campaign 245

THE STORY OF THE

THIRTY-SECOND REGIMENT

MASSACHUSETTS INFANTRY.

I.

IN GARRISON.

THE story of the 32d Massachusetts Infantry was, of course, in most respects like that of others, but not in all. The immortal Topsy thought she was not made, but "'spect she growed." So our regiment was not made a regiment at the start, but it grew to be one. Other battalions from New England gathered into camps and acquired their preliminary education among neighbors, and cheered by the presence of visitors, who looked on and admired their guard-mountings at morning, and their dress-parades at evening; and these hardened into soldiers by a rough experience in mud or dust on the line of the Potomac, while our beginning was in a walled fort, on a bleak island, isolated even from the visits of friends, and under the most exact discipline of *ante-bellum* regular-army rule.

Fort Warren, which was our cradle, is the outpost of Boston, and it was very nearly, but not entirely, completed when the war broke out. Until 1861 it had never been occupied as a military post. The 12th and 14th Massachusetts had been in occupation of the island while the organization of those battalions was in progress, during the summer of that year, and when they left, the post was somewhat hurriedly prepared for the reception of prisoners, a large number having been captured in North Carolina by the column under General Burnside.

Early in the autumn of the year 1861 Colonel Justin E. Dimmock was assigned to the command at Fort Warren. At the first outbreak of the rebellion this patriotic officer, fortunately for the cause of the Union, was in command at Fort Munroe, and resisting every attempt made upon his loyalty, he held that important post for the government under whose flag he had fought, and in whose service he had passed his active life.

As the war progressed Fort Munroe became a great centre for the operations of the army, and the duties required of its commandant were too severe for a man of Colonel Dimmock's age and infirmities, and he was transferred to the more quiet scenes in Boston Harbor. A temporary garrison was detailed from the 24th Massachusetts Infantry, then in process of formation, but upon the application of Colonel Dimmock, a new battalion of four companies of infantry was raised to be used as a garrison until the exigencies of the service required their presence elsewhere, and this body of men, called the First Battalion Massachusetts Infantry, relieved the same number of companies of the 24th.

Company A, recruited in Hingham by Captain (afterward Brevet-Brigadier-General) Luther Stephenson, jr., was mustered into service November 16th, 1861, and reported for duty at the fort on the following day. Charles A. Dearborn, jr., was First Lieutenant, and Nathaniel French, jr., Second Lieutenant.

Company B, recruited in Concord, Massachusetts, by Captain (afterward Brevet-Brigadier-General) George L. Prescott, was mustered in November 15th, 1861. Cyrus L. Tay, First Lieutenant, and Isaiah F. Hoyt, Second Lieutenant.

Company C, recruited in Boston by Captain Jonathan Pierce, was mustered in November 16th, 1861. Joseph Austin, First Lieutenant, and Robert Hamilton, Second Lieutenant.

Company D was recruited in Gloucester, and was almost entirely composed of fishermen and sailors. It was commanded by Captain James P. Draper. The late Adjutant-General James A. Cunningham was First Lieutenant, and Stephen Rich, Second Lieutenant.

These companies were rapidly recruited, and were immediately despatched to their post, no time being allowed for drill, and hardly time to say good-bye. It may be presumed that when they reported, their discipline was nothing, and their ideas of military order exceedingly crude.

Perhaps this was more particularly the case with
Company D, which, as we have already said, was
composed almost entirely of Gloucester fishermen,—
or it may have been the excessive hospitality of the
friends of that company, that led to a little scene immediately upon its arrival.

The more jovial of the soldiers were weeded out
at the landing, and quietly deposited in the guard-
house; the remainder were marched into the fort,
and soon after to the cook house, where an ample
supper of soft bread and tea awaited them. A
few months later such a repast would have been
hailed as the height of luxury, but by the raw sailor-
soldiers it was now regarded with contempt. The
loaves, instead of being devoted to their proper use
as the staff of life, were converted into missiles, and
the air was alive with them,—the dim evening light
favoring an impartial distribution.

In the midst of the racket, Colonel Dimmock appeared upon the scene, lantern in hand, and immediately received plump in the head one of the finest
of the loaves, which, with a refinement of ingenuity,
had been dipped in hot tea. The scene which followed was one not easily to be forgotten. The out-
raged old soldier dashed in among the turbulent
men, and by his habit of command at once over-
awed and controlled them. Ordering them into a
line, throwing some into position apparently by main
strength, he passed along the ranks, throwing his
light into each face until he came to the real culprit,
six solid feet of man and tar, whose face declared

his guilt. Seizing the burly giant by the arm, the old colonel fairly dragged him out of the casemate, as if he had been a child; but when the man had humbled himself sufficiently, protesting that " he didn't mean anything," the commandant dismissed him after a brief but forcible lecture on discipline, and an injunction to beware of any second offence.

Late in November the battalion organization was completed by the appointment of the Field and Staff, Francis J. Parker, Major; Charles K. Cobb, Adjutant; and George W. Pearson, Quartermaster; and the Major assumed command December 2d, 1861.

The Post-Commander, Colonel Justin E. Dimmock, was also Colonel of the First United States Artillery, and the headquarters of the regiment was with him; but with the exception of the excellent band of the regiment, there were none other of its officers or men at the post.

Fort Warren at this time was occupied as a depot for Confederate war and state prisoners—the former consisted mainly of some 800 men, captured in North Carolina, and included also a number of Confederate officers, among whom were Commodore Barron and Colonel Pegram; and among the latter were the Confederate ambassadors, Mason and Slidell, Mayor Brown, Chief of Police Kane of Baltimore, and others.

The first duty to be taught and learned under such circumstances was guard duty, and that was no holiday work. The daily detail consisted of about

seventy-five men, and was divided into the interior
and exterior guard. During the daytime a line of
sentinels enclosed a space in front of the prisoners'
quarters, within which they were permitted to exercise, and these sentinels at retreat were drawn in to
the casemate entrances. Guards were also placed
at the sally-port and postern, and near the staircases leading up to the ramparts. Outside, a picket
line entirely surrounded the fortifications; watch
being kept not only to prevent escape from within,
but also to forbid the approach of boats from the sea
or the shore.

Such duty on a bleak island, exposed to the terrible cold and storms of a New England winter, was
no pastime. Occasionally some of the outposts
would be untenable by reason of the dash of waves,
and often inspection and relief of the posts was
effected with great difficulty because of the icy condition of the ground. In the most severe storms
the guard was replaced by patrols, each of two men,
who walked the line, one patrol being despatched
every fifteen or twenty minutes.

One dark howling night the sentinel, on post
near what was called the grave-yard, reported to
the officer that a white form had twice passed
between him and the fort, and upon close questioning the soldier admitted that he had not challenged,
because he feared it was a ghost. There was considerable stir, in and outside the fort, until an inspection had shown that no prisoner had escaped and
no intruder could be found.

The sentinel was allowed two hours of extra
guard duty, and an order was posted at the guard
house denouncing severe punishment in any future
case where ghosts were allowed to pass a beat without challenge and arrest.

*　　*　　*　　*　　*　　*　　*　　*　　*　　*

Inasmuch as many who will read these pages may
never have seen the inside of a fort, a few words
descriptive of Fort Warren, may not be amiss.

The Fort proper is constructed almost entirely of
hewn granite. The area enclosed is not far from
six acres, of which the parade ground occupies five.
The general form of the area is a pentagon, but at
each of its five angles a bastion projects in such
manner that every portion of the ditch which sur-
rounds the walls, can, in case of need, be reached
by musketry and howitzers from the casemates.

This area is surrounded by casemated walls,
which are in fact huge bomb-proof buildings,
structures of stone with heavy arches of brick to
support the great mass of earth which is required to
protect them from shells thrown from mortars. In
these casemates are quarters for the officers and
men of the garrison, magazines for ammunition,
storehouses for all manner of supplies, a hospital of
generous dimensions, a huge cistern for water, an
ice-house, cook, and mess-room, besides space for a
large battery of heavy guns facing towards the sea.
Some of these vaulted chambers are lighted through
the outer walls by means of embrasures calculated
for howitzers, or by loop-holes intended for defence

by musketry. Others look out upon the parade
ground, and have upon that face the appearance of
stone dwellings of one storey, entered by ordinary
doorways, and lighted through spacious windows.
Those which occupy the northwest side of the
parade are of two stories, one being below the level
of the interior grade. These are for use as officers'
quarters, and during the war, those which are
entered from the doors nearest to, and on either side
of the entrance arch, were occupied by the civilians
and officers among the prisoners confined in the
fort.

The interior depth of the casemates, from the
inner to the outer wall, does not vary much from
sixty feet, giving ample space, equal indeed to the
depth of a large city residence. The barracks for
the soldiers are divided into rooms, generally about
sixty by twenty feet, and during a part of the war
many of them were assigned to the enlisted men
who were prisoners.

A full garrison for Fort Warren would be not far
from twenty-five hundred men, and that number
could be quartered in the casemates.

Above these buildings are the ramparts, on which
the chief part of the armament is placed, and these
ramparts are walled in by a parapet of about five feet
in height, of very thick masonry, intended to protect the men while working the guns, from the fire
of an enemy. These ramparts are now provided
with a full armament of ten inch and fifteen inch
guns, placed as near together as convenience in

working would permit, but in our day the greater part of the guns were four inch and thirty-two pounders, the casemate battery alone, consisting of eight inch columbiads.

The entire equipment of the Fort comprises over three hundred of these heavy guns, of which some seventy may always be concentrated upon any one point of the channel which they defend. Outside, and immediately surrounding the walls of the casemated fort is a fosse, or ditch, some fifty feet in width, and outside of this are other defences, (which outwardly, are earthworks,) including an exterior curtain on the north, a ravelin on the south, and a water battery on the northwest, the whole composing in fact a fortress of great strength, even in these days of iron-clads and great guns.

To one who thoroughly explores the Island there will recur vivid reminiscences of the mysterious castles of romance and of history. He will find here a sally-port, a postern, a drawbridge, and a portcullis. Here, too, are passages under ground and in the walls; turret staircases, huge vaulted apartments, and safe and dark dungeons, the ways to and through which may be set down upon the plans of the engineer corps, but are familiar to no living man. One can be easily bewildered among the crooks and turns, the ups and downs of the corridors, and it needs only a dark and windy night to make almost real the romantic descriptions of the Castle of Udolfo, with its clanging sounds of chains, its sweeping gusts of air, its strange moanings and howlings, and the startling noise of some sudden clang of a shutting door reverberating among the arches.

More than twelve years had passed since the 32d Regiment left Fort Warren for more stirring scenes, when the writer for the first time since that day, again visited the Island.

Escaping for a time from the courteous hospitality of the officers of the post, he started alone through the once accustomed scenes. Grim visaged war had smoothed his wrinkled front. There were no sentinels to challenge or salute; no familiar faces in the well-remembered quarters. Even the uniforms were changed; officers seemed to be wearing sergeants' stripes on their trousers, and unknown ornaments on their shoulders. There were women about the landing, newspapers in the guard-house (!), and a peaceful fishing pole and tackle leaned quietly against the sole survivor of all our sentry boxes.

The doorways to the officers' casemates were shielded from the hot sun by gaily painted, veranda-like porches, about which shrubs and vines, with bright foliage and blossoms, glistened in the sunlight, and in the very room where erstwhile Mason and Slidell pursued the warlike game of poker, and spat upon the bare flooring, there was a most lady-like parlor, with carpets, mirrors, and an attractive-looking case of book-shelves, well loaded with seemly books.

Again was paced the line of our outposts. Every step awakened old memories — every pebble seemed a friend; but there was no ice upon the glacis or the "shelf" at post eighteen, and instead of the cold winds, came grateful breezes from the sea, which no longer leaden in color dashed against the rock, but blue and smooth basked in the hot noonday, and laughingly rippled on the beach. It would have been a sad walk but for the beauty of the summer scenes—it would have been a joyous one but for clinging memories.

During the time of our stay in garrison at Fort Warren, the battalion was increased to six companies by the addition of Companies E and F, recruited during the winter.

Company E was raised in the Old Colony by Captain Cephas C. Bumpus. First Lieutenant, Josiah C. Fuller; Second Lieutenant, Lyman B. Whiton. The Company was mustered into service December 7th, 1861, and joined immediately.

Company F was enlisted in Boston, also by Captain Bumpus, who was detailed for the duty, and was mustered in about the first of March, 1861, its officers being, Captain, James A. Cunningham; First Lieutenant, Charles K. Cobb, (Adjutant); Second Lieutenant, William H. Gertz.

The breaking in of the men was upon the regular-army system; first each man was "set up" by himself, then the drill was in squads, in increasing numbers, and afterward in company and battalion. When the weather was such as absolutely to forbid out-of-door drill, the men were taught in the school of artillery, and practiced on the great guns in the casemate battery.

The most exact discipline was necessarily maintained, and as soldierly discipline is only to be obtained by close attention to minutiæ—not even things apparently trifling were neglected. The fact that one button of a soldier's overcoat was not fastened, was noted and the parade was stopped until the defect was remedied. No soldier was allowed to sit in the presence of an officer. The regulation salutes proper to each rank were required and paid by officers and men, sentinels and the guard. Adhering to the letter of the regulations, our manual was that of Scott, because we were armed with muskets, not rifles. Every nook and corner of every barrack and bunk, and every portion of the dress of every officer and man, must at all times be satisfactory to the keen and critical eye of an "old army" Colonel.

All of this was needed to make perfect soldiers, and all of it was readily accepted and observed by the men, more than nine-tenths of whom were American born, in order that they might become good soldiers. Singularly enough it was more difficult to bring the officers to exact the honors due to rank, than the soldiers to yield them.

Army officers often expressed their surprise at the rapidity with which a command so essentially native, was brought to the extreme of army discipline, and almost without punishment. This result was a complete proof that intelligent Americans can be brought into a state of thorough and exact discipline more readily, by reason of their intelligence, than the uneducated immigrants who were once thought to make better soldiers because of their comparative ignorance. Of course there were occasional extra hours of guard duty for men returning from leave on shore—people on the mainland were so very hospitable—but rarely was any more serious correction requisite.

There was one case, a second offence perhaps, where the sinner was put on special log duty, and he has since declared that it was sufficiently severe to keep him dry for six months. Two or three sticks of four-foot firewood, not excessively large, but good fair size, were placed in the bastion near the officers' quarters, and as many more at the extreme end of the parade, near the postern. The offender was ordered to shoulder a billet from one bastion, and to carry it in "common time" to the other; there to lay it down, and taking up another, to return over his beat and deposit it at the place of departure—and so on for several hours. The punishment consisted, not in the laborious character of his occupation, but in the fact that he knew it was useless labor, and that everybody else knew it also. The occasional inquiries or remarks of comrades about the profits of the carrying trade in fuel, may very likely have aggravated the penalty.

Bearing in mind the fact that Great Britain was wroth at the seizure of the rebel envoys, and connecting that with the other fact that a large fleet of British men-of-war was gathering at Halifax, it seemed possible that a demonstration might be made for the recovery of the lost plenipos; and it was, perhaps, natural that some interest should be felt as to our ability to repel attack, or to endure blockade, and, of course, as to the amount of our stores of food and ammunition.

Perhaps it was just as well for us at this time that no enemy appeared, for our stock of fixed ammunition consisted of thirty rounds, borrowed from Fort Independence. We were unable to salute the Governor, on his visit, for want of powder, and months passed before our magazines contained shot, shell, or powder in any more respectable quantity.

The duties of our battalion at Fort Warren were of course entirely military. The affairs of the prisoners were administered by Colonel Dimmock and his staff,—one of whom inspected the quarters every day to see that all of the prisoners were present; and all their correspondence and communications with the outside world passed under the eye of the post officers.

No prisoners could be better cared for or more considerately treated. Each was allowed the full ration of a soldier, and was even allowed to commute the ration and expend the money for other food. A liberal portion of the lading of the steamer, whose daily visit was our only tie to the continent, was made up of purchases and gifts for these guests of the nation, and their messes were always abundantly supplied both with solids and fluids.

Mr. Mason was a portly gentleman, evidently accustomed to good living; rather jovial in his ap-

pearance, and courteous in his manner. He took matters very easily, and seemed in no haste to depart. Mr. Slidell, on the contrary, a lean and dyspeptic looking man, was fretful and impatient, and evidently chafed much under his confinement.

Mayor Brown, of Baltimore, whose case was one of those which perhaps could not be entirely avoided, of unjust confinement, was always easy and bland in manner, and genial and affable to all about him, contrasting very decidedly with Kane, the Chief of the Baltimore Police, who was a thoroughly ugly specimen of a Maryland rebel.

Later on we had the pleasure, for a time, to see with us General Tilghman, a merry, happy-go-lucky officer, and General Buckner, an excellent specimen of the ramrod soldier.

The two last named were, for a time, by special order from Washington, kept in solitary confinement, —that is to say, each was assigned to a separate apartment in the basement of the commandant's quarters. Their rooms and their doors were exactly opposite each other, and a sentinel was posted in the passage to prevent escape or communication between them. Occasionally, when the weather was warm, they were allowed to leave their doors open, and on one such occasion the officer on his rounds at night found the sentinel slumbering on the floor, and the *solitary* prisoners having a good time together in one of the apartments. That soldier was not allowed to sleep a great deal for the next day or two.

Colonel Dimmock declined an earnest invitation to pass Christmas eve and day in Boston, because,

as he said, he knew that among southern people it
was held to be a Christian duty to be royally drunk
at yule tide, and his presence might be important.
It was our impression that no violence was done to
southern principles on that occasion.

The first day of January, 1862, came, bringing
with it a brisk gale of wind from the eastward, thick
lead-colored clouds, and occasional dashes of rain.
It brought also a great excitement to our humdrum
community. A steam tug came to the wharf early
in the morning, and its sole passenger, a civilian,
was escorted to the quarters of the Commandant;
then the Colonel went in person to the quarters of
our Major, and there was a conference; then the
drum-call sounded for parade earlier than usual, and
by so many extraordinary occurrences our population was " convulsed with excitement." Very soon
everybody knew that an order had been received
for the release of Mason and Slidell. There was a
great stir among the first circles of the prisoners,
and we afterward learned that they and the envoys
imagined that honors and salutes would be paid upon
their departure. But in this expectation they were
destined to disappointment. The precautions of
Colonel Dimmock entirely prevented any semblance
of honors, and even suppressed the exhibition of
such curious interest as would naturally have attended the incident.

Two sections of men, specially detailed, were so
posted as to prevent any person ascending to the
ramparts. The battalion was kept under arms and

exercise upon the parade, and the prisoners were notified that unless they would give their parole not to make any noisy demonstrations, they would be confined to their casemates. And so it happened, that, except a noiseless waving of hands and handkerchiefs from their fellow-prisoners, the envoys received no attention from any one. As they passed out from the fort, escorted only by the Commandant, the officer of the day, and the agent of the State Department, the battalion stood in line of battle, with their backs to the envoys, with ordered arms and at parade rest. As they passed the guard house, the guard also stood at parade rest, Colonel Dimmock having waived the salute due to his rank, for fear that it might be claimed as an honor to his departing guests.

The prolonged gale had caused the tide to flood the wharf, so that it was not easy or pleasant to pass over it to the tug boat. When underweigh not one person, except the sentinels on the outposts, could be seen on the island, and the driving rain and wind soon forced the passengers to seek the shelter of the cabin, which they found profusely decorated with the American flag. It is said that Mason spat and Slidell swore the whole of the rough voyage to Provincetown, in which secluded harbor a British man-of-war received them from the tug, without any demonstration, and at once put to sea.

Among the prisoners at the fort was one Keene (?), who was kept in close confinement in a small, triangular room in the casemates, the only light to

c

which came through a loophole in the masonry. He
was a sailor, and it was said that he had attempted to
blow up the frigate *Congress* with all on board, with
which horrible design he had enlisted in our navy.
He was offered greater liberty if he would promise
not to attempt an escape, but the offer was declined.
Afterward he refused to take an oath of allegiance
as the only condition for his release, and he was
probably let loose at last without condition.

We had a great desire to ascertain what time
would be required for the formation of the battalion
in case of night alarm, but Colonel Dimmock would
not permit the beating of the long-roll for a mere
experiment, because false alarms were forbidden
by the regulations. Happily that invaluable code
placed no restriction on the hours for parade, and
when, by the absence of the Colonel, our Major was
left in command of the post, the information was
obtained.

Tattoo had been sounded, roll-call was over,
lights in the barracks were all out, and the men in
bed and generally asleep. An extra guard was
quietly posted in front of the prisoners' quarters,
and a verbal message summoned the officers to headquarters.

When all were assembled they were told that it
was desirable to know how soon, under such circumstances, the battalion could be assembled, properly
equipped and ready for duty.

The order was given at eight minutes past ten, —
the officers were obliged to equip themselves and to

turn out, form and march their men on to the parade; but in less than five minutes the line was formed, with three-fourths of the whole force present. The inspection showed few deficiencies (one man, to be sure, forgot his trousers), and the experiment was quite satisfactory.

We were not without occupation, nor even without our amusements through the long winter. The officers were fully occupied, in the intervals of duty, in boneing over the tactics. To learn and teach both the infantry and artillery manual, as well as battalion movements, and at the same time to perform the various duties of the post, implied no great amount of leisure,—on the part of the officers at least. But time was found for an occasional evening entertainment, including one or two excellent concerts.

One evening there was a musical soiree in the quarters of Mr. Buell, one of the post staff, and two or three of the prisoners were present by his invitation; among them was Colonel Pegram, of Virginia, who, being invited to sing, complied, and to the surprise of everybody selected the disloyal song, "My Maryland," which he sang well to his own guitar accompaniment. When he stopped, there ensued for a minute or two an absolute and ominous silence, which was broken by our Captain Draper, who, with his ringing voice, began the patriotic song, "Vive l'America." The chorus was taken up by all the Union officers present, singing perhaps with more fervor than accuracy:—

"United we stand, divided we fall,
Union forever — freedom to all,
Throughout the wide land our motto shall be
Vive l'America, land of the free." ·

At the close of the song Colonel Pegram complimented the singing, and frankly apologized for his
discourtesy.

At times the interior of the fort seemed better
adapted for use as a skating rink than as a parade-
ground. In the worst of such times the dress-
parades were omitted, and guard-mounting took
place in the casemates; but the marching of the
reliefs over glare ice, in a high wind, did not convey
the idea of an exact military movement.

One of the men, engaged on a job of repairs,
loaded up a light hand-cart with five or six boards,
and essayed to push the load before him from the
north-west bastion to the opposite side of the fort,
while the ice was as smooth as a mirror, and a northwest gale blowing furiously. It was a slow process
at the start, but when the team emerged from under
the lee of the walls, the gale seized the whole concern, boards, cart, and man, and sent them in
detached parties, whirling over the ice field.

Our winter was a new experience to the North
Carolina men, and no doubt they have yet great
stories to tell of the snow and ice and cold, of a sea-
coast everywhere bounded by rocks, and of a .
country where the woods were not all pines. And
no doubt their hearers try to look as though they
believed it all, but mutter, possibly, some truisms
about soldiers' stories.

One day in February, 1862, just after the mail-boat had left the fort not to return until the next day, we saw all about us on the main land indications that some joyful incident had occurred. All day long flags were profusely displayed and salutes were fired up and down the coast, and at night the horizon sparkled with fireworks and bonfires. For twenty-four hours we were left to guess at the cause of this rejoicing, but at last we too heard of the capture of Fort Donelson and had our celebration.

We always gave Colonel Dimmock credit for an act of kind thoughtfulness on this occasion. When the news came he remembered that he had an engagement "on shore," and announced that he should be absent for a day. "Of course," he said, " you will fire a salute, and I don't like the sound of great guns." The fact was, no doubt, that he feared that his presence might be a restraint upon our joviality, and for that reason he took himself away. There had been no talk of anything except the salute, but as he left the fort he turned to the Major and said, in his absent-minded way, " By the by, Major, when the men are allowed a little unusual liberty, unusual discretion is needed on the part of the commanding officer, you know."

From the time required to prepare for that salute, it was evident that the *Alabama* might have steamed up the channel and into Boston harbor before we could have brought any guns to bear upon her, but at noon the guns were manned and the salute was fired. While the preparations were in progress, the band-

master of the 1st Artillery presented himself at headquarters to ask a favor.   The last gun he had fired
was the last from Fort Sumter, and he now requested permission to fire the first gun of the salute
for the victory.   Of course he was allowed to do so,
and he was cheered as he went to his station.

The Colonel was very chary of that band and we
had never had any benefit from it ; but the Post being
pro tempore under the command of our Major, they
were turned out and made useful.   All drills were
suspended for the day.   The men, in small parties,
were allowed to stroll outside the walls.   Some
luxuries were added to the ration.   The band played
and the men danced to its music and skylarked
generally.   At night there was an illumination,
masquerading, and singing, and for once tattoo did
not sound at the time set down in the orders.

A week later a detachment of prisoners from Fort
Donelson was added to our establishment, mostly
long, gaunt men, given to wearing sombrero hats,
and chewing tobacco.   With this party came Generals Buckner and Tilghman.

In February too, the last of the private soldiers,
held at the fort as prisoners of war, were sent south
to be exchanged.   When the transport was ready
for the embarkation, four negroes, servants to
officers who were about to return home, asked to
be allowed to accompany their masters.   Colonel
Dimmock, becoming satisfied that they preferred
to go back to North Carolina, consented to allow
them to do so, but took the not unnecessary pre-

caution to have other evidence of the fact that they returned to slavery on their own motion, sending them with his orderly to the Major with the request that he would examine the "boys" and satisfy himself as to whether they went of their own accord—which they certainly did.

As good-weather days became more frequent, our battalion, now of six companies, settled down more regularly to its work. At the request of our commanding officer the full code of discipline, with no abatement because we were volunteers, was the rule by which we were governed, and no one was more surprised at the result than Colonel Dimmock.

With the end of April, 1862, we had fairly drilled through the book, and on the first day of May the battalion was reviewed by Governor Andrew, and exercised in battalion movements in presence of the Governor and a staff which had become critical in military movements. At the close of the parade, Colonel Dimmock, who was not wont to abound in compliments, publicly congratulated the Major as the commander of a body of thoroughly-disciplined soldiers.

The Union armies were now everywhere victorious, and at the North we expected every day to hear that the rebels had come to that "last ditch." Wearying of the monotony, and in expectation of an early peace, the Major resigned, and on the 2d of May was relieved from duty and returned to his business life. To him the parting was unexpectedly trying, but people cannot be shut up together for five months without loving or hating each other.

For weeks the duty went on, the command devolving upon Captain Stephenson, and the warm spring weather and longer days were improved to the utmost in keeping away the possibility of rust.

The official acceptance of the Major's resignation had been received at the Post, but had not been promulgated, when on the night following Sunday, May 25th, at an hour or more past midnight, a steam tug landed him at the Post, and a half hour later everybody was awake, and the fort was alive with the news that since the last sundown the 1st Battalion had become the 32d Massachusetts Infantry — that Major Parker was promoted to the Lieutenant Colonelcy — that marching orders had been received — that Banks had been driven down the Shenandoah Valley — that Washington was menaced by the forces under Stonewall Jackson — that the country had again been summoned to the defence of the capital — that at last our time had come.

Whoever may read these sketches will pardon so much digression as will be required to describe one of the critical scenes of those exciting days. Sunday evening, after ten o'clock, this writer was sitting in his library, having just finished the last cigar before bed-time, when there came a ring at the doorbell — one of those rings that tell a story of haste and excitement.

At the door was a messenger, who informed the Major that the Governor desired to see him without delay, and that a carriage waited his convenience.

There was a word to say to the wife above stairs — there were boots and overcoat to be donned, but in two or three minutes the carriage was whirling through the empty streets, and soon pulled up at the rear entrance to the Capitol.

In the office of the Adjutant-General was Governor Andrew, busily writing at his desk and alone. His Excellency had remembered a parting request upon the occasion of the review, that the 1st Battalion should not be allowed to go to the front under a stranger's command. The Major was shown the dispatches of the night, and in them read a story of frantic terror at Washington and earnest pleading for speedy succor. By them the Governor was, within the limits of Massachusetts, invested with all of the President's power to command the United States forces, to raise troops, to transfer garrisons, to provide supplies and transportation, and through them all ran the tones of extremest panic and most earnest entreaty for help — speedy help.

The Governor stated his intention under this authority to order away the six hundred men of the 1st Battalion and offered to reappoint the commander. The offer was of course accepted and an hour quickly passed in drawing orders and requisitions, and completing arrangements for the earliest possible departure of the command. The company of heavy artillery at Fort Independence was ordered to remove to Fort Warren, and the independent companies of Cadets were ordered there for garrison duty. There were orders, too, for levy *en masse* of

the state militia for active service, and provision
made for their equipment, subsistence, and rapid
transportation.

Officers of the Governor's and of the army staff
came and went. Red tape broke at every order,
and during this hour, as also for one nearer morning,
while everybody strove to do his utmost to accomplish results which seemed almost impossible,
Governor Andrew was the busiest of the workers,
radiant with the joy of one who possesses great
powers, and who knows that he is wielding them
effectually. All through the night came over the
wires appeals for help and for haste, and always the
Governor was cheery and full of faith, that, although
the end might be farther away than we had hoped,
that end would be our success.

＊　　＊　　＊　　＊　　＊　　＊　　＊　　＊　　＊

It was a night, too, of hard work at Fort Warren
—there were rations to be issued and cooked for the
march; there were equipments to be supplied, knapsacks to be packed, property to be turned over,
unnecessaries to be rid away, and last letters to be
written; but all was done before the relief garrison
reported. At noon on Monday the regiment was
relieved, and for the last time passed out of the
sally-port and was on the march—glad to be out of
jail, some said—glad to be moving to the front;
all desiring to see that actual war for which they
had passed through long and careful training, and
anxious as new troops can be, for a share in the
realities of the campaign.

And so, embarking on the ferry-boat *Daniel Webster*, we left Fort Warren, our cradle, with cheers for the good old Colonel, and with all the verses of the John Brown chorus ringing from six hundred throats to the accompaniment of our own drum corps.

II.

ON OUR OWN HOOK.

SUNDAY, May 25th, 1862, the sun went down on a people rejoicing in the confident expectation of coming victory and an early peace. That sun next rose on a population deeply agitated with news of military disaster, but more warlike and more determined than ever. The appeals of the War Office at Washington, and the summons of our own Governor, met with an enthusiastic response; the militia flocked to the rendezvous in Boston, and the city scenes were almost a repetition of the Lexington Day of the previous year.

Not knowing that the Regiment was expected to appear on the Common, but knowing that our orders were urgent, the 32d marched by the most direct route through the city and to the railway, its wide platoons occupying the full space in the widest streets, bearing no flag, marching to its own field music, everywhere cheered by the excited populace, and drawing attention and applause by its unpretentious but soldierly appearance.

At the Old Colony station, where a train was waiting, we stacked for the last time our smooth-bore muskets, and turned them over to Quartermaster McKim. A long delay, occasioned by the unexpected celerity of our movements, gave officers and men an opportunity to exchange greetings with and take leave of their friends, of whom the vast crowd seemed chiefly to be composed.

There were meetings and partings between parents and children, husbands and wives, brothers and sisters; there were friends of the men who desired to enlist and to go with them, and others who asked brief furloughs for those they loved, that the suddenness of departure might be a little softened to those at home; but on the part of the soldiers there were no such applications. There were messages from many a quivering lip, sent to those who had not heard of the marching orders; there was grasping of hands, man with man, which meant more than tongues could say; and wives were folded by husband's arms so tenderly as may never be but either in days of early love or at the approach of final separation.

And yet there was no cloud of sadness in the scene; on every side were words of cheer and encouragement—of loving hope and patriotic devotion; and when a light-hearted soldier, whose home was so far away that none of his kin were there to say good-bye, asked if there was nobody there to kiss him, he came near being smothered by a crowd of volunteers ready to officiate, not only for his mother, but for all the rest of his female ancestry.

At last came the regimental stores, for which we had waited, and with the call for "all aboard," the last ties were broken, the last cheers were given, and the train drew slowly out from the station and from the city. But not away from tokens of good will. The country, too, was alive. Flags were streaming from every flag-staff, waving from the windows of the houses, and drooping from the spires of churches.

Men, women, and children of all ages were at cottage doors and roadway crossings, and crowded the platforms at every station, to say or wave good-bye and God-speed to the foremost of the transport trains. We were soon at Fall River, on the steamer, and weary with excitement, the men speedily turned in and slept.

For us there was next day no Broadway parade in New York city, but landing at Jersey City there was a haversack breakfast, and after some delay, another train, and we were off for Philadelphia, through a country whose people, in hamlet and in town, cheered the unknown soldiery, who all day long poured through toward the seat of war. At Philadelphia we shared the bounteous hospitality of the citizens, who provided most thoughtfully for all the troops who passed their gates. There was a long march through wide and straight streets, then another railway embarkation, and then a long, tedious, hesitating ride, reaching through the night, and it was early morning when we arrived at Baltimore and woke the drowsy people with the sound of Yankee Doodle as we marched through to the Washington railway. Here we found the 7th New

York militia waiting in the street for transportation
to the Capital. More successful than they, we
secured a train, which, after several hours, delivered us safely in Washington, where we were glad
to learn that we were the first troops to arrive on the
call of the President, and that again Massachusetts
was in the advance.

Then followed a prolonged struggle with red tape,
which would have told us, even if there had been no
other source of information, that the scare was over
and Washington safe. Before we could present our
requisitions for camp equipage, the office hours had
passed, the officials were deaf to all our entreaties,
and although we arrived as early as 2 P. M., we
were compelled that night to occupy the hard
floors of one of the railway buildings.

When we came to look about us we were surprised
to find that ours was the only infantry regiment at
Washington, and we were poor lone orphans. We
wanted tents, supplies, and a wagon train, but our
requisitions were denied, because our Brigadier General had not endorsed his approval. We attempted
to explain that we had no Brigadier, and all Staff-
dom stood aghast,—unable to take in the idea that
there could be such a thing as a regiment with no
brigadier.

Verily, we might have died of starvation but for
the kindness of Adjutant General Townsend, who
officially made a special order from the headquarters of the army, to suit our case, and personally
suggested a site near the Washington Navy Yard,

known as Camp Alexander, as a convenient locality
for our camp. The site was inspected, approved,
and speedily occupied by us, and here passed four
weeks of halcyon days. Our camp was pitched on
a high bluff overlooking the eastern branch of the
Potomac. The air was that of balmy June. No
brigadier worried us—no up-and-away orders disturbed us, and thanks to General Townsend's special order, our supplies were ample and regular.

But it was no idle time. A battalion which had
always been restricted to the limits of an island fort,
had occasion for much new practice, and the drills
went briskly on. Especially was there need for
practising in the use of legs, before marching orders
should come, and therefore, every other day the
drills of the battalion comprised also a march, growing longer day by day, until an eight-mile march
was easily accomplished.

Our evening parades became quite an attraction
for visitors. Congressmen, senators, and even cabi-
net secretaries came to be frequent guests, and the
sunshine of ladies' presence, unknown to our previous experience, gave brilliancy to our lines and
encouragement to our men.

Washington was at this time in a state of siege,
or according to our American phrase, under martial
law. The great army, which a few months earlier
had given to the district the appearance of a military camp, had moved on toward Richmond. One
column was wading up the Peninsular, one was
watching in the Shenandoah Valley, one was guard-

ing the Piedmont Gaps, while McDowell, on the banks of the Rappahannock, was waiting the turn of events, and hoping for orders to join the force under McClellan, and so on to Richmond.

The chain of detached forts about the Capital, were, however, fully garrisoned, and in the city a force of cavalry was doing the work of a provost guard. Mounted sentinels were stationed at the street corners, and detachments patrolled the outlying wards. The railway station was guarded, and passengers leaving town were obliged to pass the inspection of the soldiery. At the depots of the commissary's and the quartermaster's stores, at the entrances to hospitals, about the offices of the departments, and at the door of the Executive Mansion, sentries were posted day and night. One was rarely out of sight and hearing of officers and orderlies, as they galloped over the rough pavements or trailed their sabres on the walks, and everywhere came and went the springless supply-wagons of the army, with their six-mule teams and postilion drivers.

All this appearance of military rule and ward was no useless show. The city was full of enemies and spies. A large part of the resident population was hostile to the North. Very frequently at the approach of uniformed men, ladies gathered their skirts to prevent contaminating touch, and children shook their tiny fists and made grimaces of dislike.

If there seemed to be exceptional cases where officers were welcomed by secessionists, men or women, the attentions were apt to end in a request for aid to procure passes through our lines, or in wily cross-examination about posts or movements of the troops. There was but little tinsel; except at the barracks of the marine corps, where old traditions were preserved, there were no epaulettes, no chapeaux, no plumes, but everything spoke of real war service.

He who visits Washington now will find it hard to realize that that beautiful capital is the same as the dust and mud-covered town of 1862. He who has known it only as the beleaguered city of the war, would almost fail to recognize it in its changed condition.

It seemed at times as if we had been lost or forgotten by the war department; but an occasional order, or the call for some report, betrayed a semi-consciousness of our existence. None of the authorities could take in the idea that we had only six companies, and when a funeral escort was wanted for the body of Lieutenant-Colonel Palmer, of the engineers, the order came to detail six companies, under a Lieutenant-Colonel, for that duty, and our commanding officer thereupon detailed himself and his full command.

This escort was, in all our history, the only instance of show duty. Our newly-joined Assistant-Surgeon Faxon, with such daring as could come only from raw ignorance, volunteered to take the compliments of our commander to the General commanding the Marine Corps, and to ask for the loan

of his celebrated band. Whether the General was stunned by our impudence or flattered by the Doctor's blandishments, may never be known, but the request was complied with, and our march through the crowded city was made dazzling by the great band, with their plumed caps, scarlet coats, white trowsers, and gorgeous equipments.

Every point of military etiquette was observed in the ceremonial; the command was in the best of condition, and we heard with great satisfaction the favorable comments from the crowds that thronged our way. " It takes the regulars," " volunteers never could do that," etc. And no doubt as we marched back to our camp of spacious tents, with the full assurance of ample rations prepared by company cooks awaiting our arrival, our breasts swelled with undue pride, for we saw in the future no premonitions of the tattered and hungry crew, who bearing our name and number, were to assist in puddling down the sacred soil of Virginia.

Within the limits of our camp was a small and old cottage house, which being entirely unoccupied, we took for our hospital use. Although nearly worth- less for any purpose, the owner was hunted up and the endeavor was made to come to a settlement with him and pay rent during its occupancy, but the pro- prietor declined even to name a price, giving as his reason that he could get more by making a claim for it before the department, after we were gone.

At this hospital we first lost a man from our ranks by death. Hiram Varney of Gloucester, a plucky fellow, although too ill to have left the Fort, prevailed upon the post surgeon to allow him to go with the Regiment, but worn with the excitement and fatigue of the march, he fell into typhus fever and died. He was a soldier to the last. So long as he could raise his hand, he endeavored to salute his officers who came to the cotside, and when told of approaching death, he regretted that it had not been his fate to meet it in battle.

There were other incidents not so lugubrious. The waters of the Branch washed the foot of the bluff on which our camp was pitched, and when the days grew exceeding hot, Surgeon Adams advised that bathing should be prohibited through the heat of the day. Accordingly an order was published, appointing the hours for morning and evening bathing, and forbidding it at other times.

At noon one blistering hot day, two men being overtempted by the cool waters, were in the act of enjoying a stolen bath, when the sergeant with a file of the guard appeared and ordered the bathers to the shore. Upon coming to land, they found to their disgust that their clothing had preceded them to the guard tent. Attended by the sergeant and his men, the culprits were marched *in puris* up the bluff and through the whole length of the parade ground, running the gauntlet of the jokes and gibes of their comrades, who turned out in force to enjoy the exhibition.

For a day or two after our arrival the cows of our secession neighbors were very troublesome. Turned out by their owners after milking in the morning, a herd of some twenty-five or thirty head fed through the day along the waste grounds of that part of Washington City, and returned at evening to their cribs. Both going and coming they habitually passed through our lines, and about among the tents, causing some trouble to the police guard, and much annoyance to the men. Sentinels could not leave their posts to chase cows, and no provision was to be found in the tactics or regulations applicable to this case. A provision was therefore invented. At noon a notice was posted at the guard tent, stating that thereafter it might be presumed that any cows found within the limits of the camp were sent thither by their owners, in order that the men should supply themselves with fresh milk.

When the herd returned that evening there was exhibited a scene which defies description. Upon each cow there attended upon the average about five men, who with soothing words and quieting gestures, sought an opportunity to drain the happy beeves! A view of the camp was one of a confusing medley of cows, and of men with tin cups, slowly and quietly but almost continually waltzing about in every direction. All their exertions must have resulted in a considerable success, for the herd troubled us no more.

The guard served with loaded rifles, and when relieved were marched to a convenient spot by the waterside, where they emptied their guns one by one, firing at a target; and to encourage careful prac-

tice, he who made the best shot was allowed a furlough for the rest of the day. It was of course a
matter of interest to the officers to watch the practice
and the improvement of the men. On one occasion
after the guard practice was ended, the Colonel
desiring to test the new pieces, took a rifle from the
sergeant, and by some accident his bullet hit the
bull's eye of the target. He was complimented and
perhaps a little surprised by the unanimous shout
from the old guard, "give him a furlough."

The East Branch here must have been not far from
a quarter of a mile wide. Our shore, as has been
stated, was a high bluff, but the opposite bank was
a low interval, cultivated as a market garden, and
near the river stood the unpretentious cottage of the
cultivator. As the colonel sat one day at his tent
door, in such position that the edge of the bluff
showed in sharp relief against the blue waters of the
branch, there appeared coming up over the cliff,
escorted by a corporal, a semblance of Neptune aris-
ing from the Sea. It was after all only the garden
farmer from over the river. He had crossed in his
punt, and his resemblance to Neptune was owing in
part to his sailor-like form and hat, but more to the
precaution he had taken to bring his paddle along
with him.

His errand at headquarters was to complain that
the rifle balls at the time of target practice had
a disagreeable way of glancing over the water
and whistling about his premises, and he asked
meekly if this could not be avoided, as it "made the

women-folks nervous." Of course his wish was
granted, and thereafter the guard discharged their
rifles at a target in the bank on our side of the water.
This compliance with his request resulted in a
second appearance of our Neptune, who at this time
brought two boxes of choice strawberries as a present to the commanding officer, and an expression of
his thanks, to which he added the statement that
there never had been such a regiment encamped
near him,—"they were all gentlemen." We wondered what kind of troops had preceded us, that we
rose so high in his good graces merely because we
refrained from shooting at his women-folks,—but the
berries were thankfully accepted and warmly appreciated in the mess.

It was about this time that this delicious berry
became so plentiful that three hundred quarts were
issued as a special ration to the men.

June 24, 1862. Orders were received to move
over to Alexandria, where a new brigade comprising
the 32d was to be organized; the order stated that the
Regiment would be met at Alexandria by a staff
officer who would conduct us to our camping ground.

Alexandria being a township about ten miles in
length, the order was rather indefinite, but we
marched to the town where we found no brigadier,
no brigade, and no staff officer, and thereupon we
proceeded to make an excursion through the township in search of one of them. We soon found an
aide-de-camp who conducted us to the locality intended, and pointed out the ground assigned to us,
which was half a mile from any water.

This, our first real march, is worthy of notice, as being almost the only one which was made without loss by straggling, and the only one made in accordance with army regulations.

Six months afterward, when the allowance of wagons was only three to each regiment, we laughed as we remembered the twenty-three wagons which were required for this first movement of ours. Our route covered sixteen miles, when, if the order had been decently explicit, only eight miles would have been required, but we soon learned that it was one of the customs of the service to make the orders as blind as possible.

Before nightfall our camp was made and our guards posted. No military authority had ever notified us of a countersign, we therefore as usual made our own, and consequently before morning bagged a half dozen of the officers from the neighboring forts, who were ignorant of it.

A Rhode Island Regiment, (Colonel Bliss',) and one from Pennsylvania arrived the next day, and for several days we were in constant expectation of a brigadier, but before he turned up, June 29th, an order came for the 32d to be mustered early on the 30th by its commanding officer, and thereafter to proceed forthwith to Alexandria, where transportation would be in readiness to take the command to Fort Monroe. At 11 A. M., we were in the street at Alexandria with all our baggage train, but the General commanding there was drunk, the Post Quartermaster insolent, and nobody had ever heard anything about us or our transportation. After waiting until 4 P. M., receiving no orders nor even replies from Washington to our telegrams, we concluded to operate on our own hook, and when the Steamer *Hero* came to a landing near by, we took possession of her as a "military necessity," coaled her and started for our destination.

We found the aforesaid "military necessity" to be a poor shattered concern, already deeply laden with ammunition. The captain and crew were not in an amiable frame of mind at being so unceremoniously gobbled up. They refused to allow the men to make coffee at the boiler fires, and when ordered to do so, the engineers and firemen left their posts in high dudgeon; but when they found that we had a plenty of men competent to run the boat, and that it was their rations, not ours, that were stopped, they very submissively returned to their duty.

We arrived at Fort Monroe early on the 2d of July, and reported to General Dix, commanding that post. Here we heard of the seven days fighting across the Peninsula, and found the air full of exciting and contradictory rumors as to the incidents and result of the battles. Even General Dix had no precise information as to the whereabouts of General McClellan, but he knew that he wanted more men and wanted them quick, and we were directed without disembarking to proceed up the river until we found the army. Facilities were provided for cooking the neccesary rations, and early in the afternoon, after receiving repeated injunctions to take

every precaution against falling into the hands of
the enemy, we weighed anchor and steamed away
up the James.   Our heavily-laden boat could not
make the distance by daylight, and we passed the
night at anchor in the river, with steam up and a
large guard on duty, and with the early dawn were
again underweigh, in search of the army.

To this time the Regiment had practically lived by
itself; it had known nothing of generals, and not
much of army men, but the time had come when it
was to be absorbed into the army as a drop into the
ocean.

III.

ON THE PENINSULA.

IT was yet early morning when we steamed over
Harrison Bar, and saw evidences of the vicinity
of the Army of the Potomac. We had previously
met quite a number of steamboats bound down the
river, apparently heavily loaded with passengers;
and now, as the river widened out into a lake or bay,
we came upon a large fleet of various kinds of crafts,
freighted with ordnance, quartermaster's and commissary stores, some at anchor in the river, and some
hauled up to the left bank unloading their freight.
The river banks were too high to enable us to see
beyond, but all along them were men sitting or lying
on the slopes, or bathing in the water. There were
teams of mules driven down to drink, and wagoners
using heavy whips and great oaths to persuade their
beasts to draw the loaded wains up the rough tracks,
cut diagonally into the faces of the bank.

As our steamer entered upon this stirring scene
the musicians were ordered to the bows of the boat,
and we moved on with our drums beating cheerily.
We passed one long wharf, reaching out into the
river, and thereabout saw a few tents and great piles

43

of stores on the shore; then pushing our reconoissance up the river, saw the army signs gradually
disappear from the banks, until at length opening a
reach of the river we could see the gunboats, the
slow booming of whose guns had been heard long
before; and here a guard-boat hailed to warn us to
go no farther.

Satisfied that the wharf, which we had passed,
was the proper place for our landing, we turned and
steamed slowly in that direction. Presently a boat
put off from the bank with an officer who signalled
for the steamer to stop, came alongside, and delivered to our Colonel a torn fragment of a second-.
hand and soiled envelope, on which, in pencil, was
scrawled the following order, our first from the
headquarters of the Army of the Potomac:—

"*To commanding officer of troops on steamer.
Land your men at once and move direct up the road,
and report to me at my headquarters, where you will
be stopped: Come up with arms and ammunition
(40 or 60 cartridges each man).*

"*This order is from General McClellan.*

"*F. J. PORTER, Brig. Gen.*"

In obedience to the order we hauled up to the
wharf, and the men being already supplied with
ammunition, but little time was lost in forming upon
the pier. Leaving there a few men to unload and
guard the baggage we moved up to the shore.

It is General Trochu who writes, that upon approaching an army from the rear in time of battle,

one always sees the same sights, conveying to one's mind the idea of a disorderly mob, and the fear of a great disaster. Our approach to the Army of the Potomac was from the rear in time of battle, and our experience confirms Trochu.

At the head of the wharf a mass of men were striving to pass the guard, hoping to get away on the steamer which had brought us. Passing them, we looked for the road up which we were ordered to move "direct." In every direction, and as far as we could see, the soil which twenty-four hours before had been covered with promising crops of almost ripened grain, was trodden into a deep clay mud,—so deep and so adhesive as, in several cases, to pull the boots and stockings from the soldiers' feet, and so universal as to have obliterated every sign of the original road. Everywhere were swarms of men in uniform, tattered and spattered with mud, but with no perceptible organization, wading through the pasty ground. On and near the river bank were open boxes, barrels, casks, and bags of provision and forage, from which each man supplied himself without the forms of requisition, issue, or receipt. Everywhere too were mule-wagon teams struggling in the mire, and the air resounded with the oaths of the drivers, the creaking of the wagons, the voices of men shouting to each other, the bray of hungry mules, and the noise of bugle and drum calls, with an accompaniment of artillery firing on land and water.

To all these were added, when we appeared, shouts, not of hearty welcome and encouragement, such as we might naturally have expected from an overtasked army to its first reinforcement, but in derision of our clean dress and exact movements— warnings of terrible things awaiting us close at hand—questions as to how our patriotism was now— not one generous cheer.

Officers and men alike joined in this unseemly behavior, and even now when we know, as we did not then, the story of the terrible days of battle through which they had passed, and the sufferings that they had patiently endured, we cannot quite forgive their unmannerly reception of a recruiting force.

Through all this we succeeded in finding General Porter's headquarters, and by his direction were guided to a position a mile or more distant, and placed in line of battle with other troops in face of a thick wood, and then learned that we were assigned to the brigade of General Charles Griffin, division of General Morell, in Fitz John Porter's, afterward known as the Fifth army corps.

As soon as we were fairly in position our Colonel sought for the brigadier. The result was not exactly what his fancy may have painted. On a small heap of tolerably clean straw he found three or four officers stretched at full length, not very clean in appearance and evidently well nigh exhausted in condition. One of them, rather more piratical look- ing than the others, owned that he was General Griffin, and endeavored to exhibit some interest in the addition to his command, but it was very reluc-

tantly that he acceded to the request that he would
show himself to the Regiment, in order that they
might be able to recognize their brigade commander.

After a time however, the General mounted and
rode to the head of our column of divisions. The
Colonel ordered "attention" and the proper salute,
and said : "Men, I want you to know and remember
General Griffin, our Brigadier General." Griffin's
address was perhaps the most elaborate he had ever
made in public. "We've had a tough time men,
and it is not over yet, but we have whaled them every
time and can whale them again."

Our men, too well disciplined to cheer in the
ranks, received the introduction and the speech, so
far as was observed, in soldierly silence, but months
afterward the General told that he heard a response
from one man in the ranks who said, "Good God ! is
that fellow a general." We all came to know him
pretty well in time, and to like him too, and some of
us to mourn deeply when he died of the fever in
Texas, after the surrender.

The officers of our Field and Staff found in the
edge of the wood just in front of the Regiment, a
spot somewhat drier than the average, and occupied it, but not without opposition. A long and
very muddy corporal was gently slumbering there,
and on waking, recognized his disturbers by their
clean apparel as new comers, and thought they
might be raw. Pointing to an unexploded shell
which lay near him on the ground, he calmly
advised the officers not to stop there, as "a good

many of them things had been dropping in all the
morning." His strategy proved unsuccessful, for
he was ranked out of his comfortable quarters and
told to join his regiment.

After all, the day passed without an engagement,
and the sound of guns gradually died away, until
near evening, when the Brigade was moved about
two miles away and bivouacked in a wood of holly
trees, the men making beds of green corn-stalks,
and going to them singing and laughing.

After the excitement of the day all slept soundly,
but before midnight the Colonel was aroused by an
orderly to receive a circular order which stated that
owing to certain movements of the enemy, commanding officers were to hold their commands on
the alert. Not knowing what commanding officers
were expected to do when they "held their commands
on the alert," the Colonel accompanied the General's
orderly to the headquarters of the 9th Massachusetts
near by, and waited while its commander was
aroused, and until he had perused the same order.
Observing that after reading it the veteran quietly
turned over and settled himself for a fresh nap, our
Colonel returned to his repose, merely taking the
precaution to have the horses saddled and bridled,
by which bit of innocent faith in orders for alert, he
lost the use of his saddle which had made an excellent pillow. The next day we received our baggage
and moved out of the wood, pitching our camp in
regulation shape.

I fear that the display of a full allowance of round
Fremont tents may have caused some heart burnings

among our neighbors, who had nothing but shelter tents. It is certain that they were still inclined to scoff at our peculiarities, and already the demoralizing effect of the prevalent negligence was felt in our ranks, for one of our captains, always before rather distinguished for the nicety of his dress, soon appeared splashed with mud from head to foot, and when asked why he did not remove it, he pleaded that it was the uniform of the Army of the Potomac.

* * * * * * * * *

Whoever, without a vast preponderance of forces, makes war to capture Richmond, must have the James River for his base of supply and must be able to control Harrison Landing.

When the campaign of the Army of the Potomac began, the iron-clad Merrimac barred access to the James, and the Army, which by way of that River might, without delay or loss, have flanked Magruder back to Malvern Hill, landed at Harrison's and operated on Richmond over a healthy and dry country, comparatively free from natural obstacles, — was compelled to resort to the narrow and tortuous Pamunkey, and to flounder among swamps and river crossings, always exposed to fight at disadvantage, and always weakened physically and mentally by the malaria of the marshes.

When, by the destruction of the Merrimac, the James was made available, the mind of General McClellan reverted to his original preference. For a long time he waited and stretched out his right wing to facilitate junction with McDowell, but when the

R

last hope of that aid had disappeared, he hastened to abandon the Pamunkey for the broader and safer James. The movement was actually in progress when Johnston attacked what was already the rear of McClellan's column. During each day of that battle-week, the trains moved and the army fought, and every night the army abandoned the scene of a successful defence to close in upon the banks of the river, where alone they could hope for the supplies which they needed and the repose they had won.

The day before we joined, these rough and grimy troops had fought at Malvern perhaps the hardest of their fights, and had won the most complete of all their victories. And now they were again in communication with the North—in posession of the very key to Richmond—holding Lee as it were by a cord from any movement North, and needing only the assistance of a tithe of the new levies to drive or flank him further south. But it pleased God that this should not be until years had passed away.

If there be on the face of the earth a place intended for breeding pestilence, the country about Harrison's and Westover was ordained to that use. One of our officers who had travelled the wide world all over, declared that the climate resembled no place except Sierra Leone on the African coast. Its reputation as an unwholesome spot is established even among the natives of Virginia, and whoever desires any additional testimony, need only to apply to one who has sweltered there through July and August.

To the natural disadvantages of the locality, were now added those many sources of sickness which always accompany an army. The effect of the climate was not only debilitating to the body, but was enervating to the will, and negligence of proper precautions against camp diseases was added to all other predisposing causes in reducing the strength of the army.

The 32d, almost fresh from the sea air of New England, suffered undoubtedly more than those regiments which had been in some degree acclimated. Almost every officer and man was affected. For weeks over one-third of the command was on the sick list, and not less than a hundred and fifty men who then left the Regiment for hospital or on sick leave, never returned to our colors.

Such a mixture of moisture and drouth, of mud and dust, cannot be conceived. The air was filled at times with an impalpable dust which was actually a visible malaria. The marsh near our camp was beautiful to see, white with its vast numbers of plants like lilies which threw up great spikes of flowers, but the excess of perfume was so sickening as but little to be preferred to the odor of carrion, which came to us when the wind changed to the westward.

Men sickened and died in a day, and the whole Regiment lost its brisk military ways and degenerated very nearly to the shiftless, listless level of the rest of the army. Drills could not be kept up, parades were discontinued, and the attention of the officers was concentrated upon the preservation of cleanliness in the camp, the improvement of the food, and the necessary duties. Here occurred the first death among our officers, for Lieutenant Nathaniel French, jr., died August 9th of the malarial fever.

Large details were made from the Regiment for guards, our reputation for that duty having become unpleasantly good. Eighty men and three officers were at one time serving as guards over the quartermaster's stores, on the river bank. It was while they were there, that enterprising John Reb. brought some field pieces down to Coggins' Point, just opposite to us on the James, and opened fire about midnight, first upon the shipping in the river, and afterward upon our camps.

Two of the officers of our detached party, after the freshness of the alarm had passed, were sitting in their shelter tent with their feet to the foe, watching as they would any pyrotechnic display, the flash of the guns, and the curves described by the burning fuses, when one of the guns was turned and discharged, as it seemed, directly at our friends, who, dodging at the same moment, struck their heads together and fell, each under the impression that the enemy's shell had struck him.

It was on this occasion that Colonel Sawtelle, the officer in charge of the transportation—our quartermaster said he was the only regular officer within his experience who could do his duty and be civil too—emerged from his tent at the sound of firing and stood upon the bank gazing silently and sorrowfully upon his defenceless fleet, among which the shells were exploding merrily. Soon his silence broke into a shout to his superior, "Look here Ingalls, if this thing isn't stopped pretty quick, the A. P. is a busted concern."

In the regimental camp a half mile away, the shelling did no serious damage, but produced some commotion. One of the officers complained that every time that he got comfortably settled for sleep, a shell would knock the pillow out from under his head; in emulation of which story, a sailor in D Company declared that he slept through the whole affair, but in the morning counted twenty-three solid shot piled up against his back, that hit but had not waked him.

Nearly two months had elapsed since we left Massachusetts with the promise that the four Companies require to complete our Regiment should be speedily recruited and forwarded, but we heard nothing of them. The home newspapers told of the 33d Regiment as being full, and of the 34th and 35th as in process of formation, but the 32d seemed to have been forgotten. The Lieutenant Colonel addressed a letter to the Governor upon the subject, and forwarded a copy of his letter to the headquarters of the Army of the Potomac. Within twenty-four hours an order was published in which, among others, was the name of our commanding officer as detailed on recruiting service. Upon application to Adjutant General Williams for an explanation of the detail, he learned that the order meant that he was to go for those four companies, and leaving Captain Stephenson, who for a long time had been Acting Major, in command, the Colonel went to Massachusetts on recruiting duty, from which duty, to the best of his knowledge, he has to this day never been relieved.

He was barely gone before Company G reported, commanded by Captain Charles Bowers—Charles O. Shepard being First Lieutenant, and Edward T. Bouvé, Second Lieutenant. When we got far enough away from the depressing effect of that infamous climate, and attained sufficient animation to joke, we used to call this Company our second battalion.

There may occur no better place than this for a brief dissertation concerning the high and deep mysteries which hung about quartermastering.

When we were at the Fort, the officers—who, by regulation, were allowed a certain number of candles per month—expressed a very unanimous preference for kerosene lamps, which had then recently come in vogue. Lamps, wicks, and oil were benignantly supplied by the quartermaster at the Post, but at the end of a month that officer presented for approval and signature, requisitions and receipts for many candles. We dreamed of a nice job at court-martial on the Q. M., but soon learned that by a fiction of the department, no light was recognized other than that of candles, and receipts given for candles covered lamps, wicks, chimneys, and oil.

Whether the Quartermasters' Department has yet discovered the use of petroleum, who can tell? Our Quartermaster Pearson never joined the Regiment after it left Massachusetts, but was detailed principally in charge of matters at the recruiting post and camp at Readville. Lieutenant Hoyt of B Company was detailed and served for several years as acting quartermaster. When he was detailed the term of his detail was of course problematical, and there was too much uncertainty, as he thought, to justify the investment required for the purchase of a horse; but he must ride. With that straightforwardness which comes from innocence and ignorance alike, a requisition was made upon the proper officer for a saddle and horse for the use of the quartermaster.

If we had stolen the military chest of the army no greater outcry could have been made; the application was rejected with contumely. For the next day or two Quartermaster Hoyt appeared to be absorbed in the study of the rules and regulations, articles of war, and circulars of his department. From this course of reading he emerged with unclouded brow and a new requisition. This time it was for an ambulance, a horse, and a harness, to which every battalion was entitled, and the articles required were promptly delivered. Two days later he returned the ambulance and harness as not wanted, and kept the horse, which was always ridden by the quartermaster; but was always known as the ambulance horse.

It is a little in advance of our main story, but it may as well be told here how Hoyt flanked the Division Quartermaster. When the regimental property was unloaded from the transport at Acquia Creek, and only the afternoon before we marched, it was found that one of our wagons was sick in a hind wheel, and as it was almost sure to break down if the wagon was loaded, our quartermaster endeavored to turn it in to the Division Quartermaster, and to obtain a sound wagon in it's place. There were plenty of new wagons in the Division depot, but the officer was ugly and refused the exchange; when it was persistently urged, the superior grew wroth and vowed vows, and told our quartermaster that he would n't get any wagon out of him, and that he might help himself if he could.

Hoyt did help himself that night by taking, under cover of the darkness, a sound wheel from a wagon in the Division train, and putting our rotten one in its place. There was a great row after we started next morning about the breaking down of a wagon, but our train was all right.

Not many days after our arrival at Harrison's Landing, July 8th, President Lincoln visited and reviewed the army. Having faith — in some respects resembling a mustard seed — we believe that he reviewed the 32d. What we know is, that after waiting in position with the whole of our division, from four o'clock in the afternoon until nine o'clock in the evening, during the last three hours of which time we mourned our delayed suppers, and pos-

sibly spoke evil of dignities, we saw in the uncer-
tain moonlight a party of horsemen ride along our
front, one of whom sat his horse like Andrew Jackson, and wore a stove-pipe hat, and then we were
allowed to go to our camp and our rations.

Where there are no newspapers, rumors are
always plenty, and the army abounded in rumors.
One day it was reported that our corps was to cross
the river and march on Petersburg; another day we
were told the army was about to move on Richmond,
and that we were to assault Fort Darling. General
Hooker made a reconoissance in the direction of
Malvern, and it was immediately reported that he
had penetrated the defences of Richmond.

For two weeks orders were received almost daily
with regard to the removal of the sick, and the dis-
posal of camp equipage and all extra baggage, and
rumors grew more and more wild and contradictory.
After the fearful ordeal of the malarial sickness, it is
not surprising that the intimation that the army was
about to enter upon a new campaign was hailed
with something akin to delight, even by those who
realized the dangers of battle, and the toil of more
active service. At last the orders came for the
movement, and it was not upon Petersburg, or Fort
Darling, or Richmond, but toward Fort Monroe.

The orders found us ready and exceedingly willing to leave a spot crowded with sad and bitter
experience, such as we can not even now recall without a thrill almost of horror.

The marches of the 32d Regiment might claim
quite as much place, if not more, in its history,

than the battles in which it took part, but they
would hardly be as attractive to the reader. At
all events the incidents of a march, exciting or not,
stand a much better chance of accurate narration
than those of a battle where haste may obscure the
memory, and passion confuse the description.

In military campaigns as in civil life, patience and
endurance will win as against courage and *élan*.
The first are the qualities of highest value in marches,
the second are those conspicuous in battle.   And it
may be safely said, that the qualities in soldiers
which make good marching, are rarer than those
which make good fighting.   At least the troops
which the General will prize the most are those which
march the best: *i. e.*, those in whom either *esprit-
du-corps* or discipline is strong enough to prevent
straggling on toilsome marches.   Those who marched
in good form, and came into bivouac at night with
full ranks were sure to be ready and available at the
moment of battle, whether they fought well or not;
and per contra, it was frequently observed that those
regiments that straggled most upon the march, were
conspicuous among the great army of "bummers"
at the rear in the time of battle, and, if engaged
with the enemy, were the first to break into rout and
dismay.

Now as the 32d Massachusetts was on many occasions rather conspicuous for good solid marching,
that fact should not be forgotten in its history.

On the morning of a march the question usually
was, " Who has the advance to-day?"   In a succes-

sion of days' marching, the regiments took turns in leading, according to an established rule. Breakfast over, the bugle sounded, first at Division-headquarters, then at brigade, and last at each regiment, everybody fell into his place, and the bugle sounded again "forward." After many halts and hitches, unless we happened to be at the head of the column, we finally swung into the regular marching gait. This was not fast, rarely exceeding three miles an hour and oftener two miles or thereabouts, including halts.

The manner and method of the march,— with its object there was seldom any disposition to meddle, — were often severely criticised both by men and officers. For instance, a day's march of which the objective point might be quite distant, say 25 or 30 miles, would be begun before daylight, and then conducted in great part as though there was no fixed intention of going any where at all. This would be a ground for grumbling. Marching out of a comfortable camp at midnight, moving only a little way, and then halting and lying round without orders for hours, then moving again at day-break at a snail's pace, without having broken our fast, and keeping on in this way until near noon, with no orders for halt and breakfast; and thus on through a whole livelong day of heat or dust, or it might be of snow or rains or chilling winds, until late in the afternoon; horses not fed or unsaddled, men with blankets and equipments on, flinging themselves on the ground at every wait as if in disgust. Here

was more ground for grumbling. At length late in
the afternoon, when patience and strength were all
but exhausted, we would strike into a pace of three
miles or more an hour, which would be kept up
hour after hour without a moment's rest.   Then
would begin the straggling, men would throw away
their overcoats and blankets as too burdensome to
carry, although the loss might be bitterly regretted
at the next bivouac, and would make their fires,
rest and cook their coffee, under the very guns of
the enemy, in defiance of danger of death or capture, and in spite of command or threats of court-
martial.   The regimental column would be reduced
to the size of a company, and the men would be found
strewed along the roadside, sick or used up, many
not rejoining their companies until the bugles
sounded "forward" on the following day.   This style
of marching was frequent in the earlier campaigns
of the Army of the Potomac, but was afterwards
much amended and improved upon.   An excellent
rule adopted at a later period was to march the column steadily for one hour, and then call a halt on
the bugle for ten or fiften minutes.   But the important point of so ordering a march that the column
should move rapidly during the cool hours of the
morning and evening, halting for an hour or two at
noon, was seldom reached.   It is presumable that in
many, perhaps in most cases, marches were made
loitering and toilsome, (as above described,) by
unavoidable and obvious causes.   The insufficiency
of the roads, there being but one, or their bad

condition, crowding the way with cattle sometimes driven in the line of march ; troops going to the rear with prisoners, or passing to the front; skirmishing with the enemy ; difficult fords, or broken bridges, or the laying of pontoons ; all these, or any of them, might cause delay. Or orders might require the troops to be hurried forward, and the march, too hastily begun, would be impeded by crowding or by the necessity of cavalry, artillery, or ammunition being sent forward.

To sketch a march is an exceedingly difficult thing because there is presented to the observer such a multitude of features, none of which can be slighted or left out ; and these features are so varied, and present themselves in such endless succession and constantly changing interest, that the mind becomes confused.

On the occasion of our first march with the Army of the Potomac, the men, in the worst possible condition to support fatigue, weakened by sickness, softened by six weeks of inaction, and enervated by a debilitating climate, were marched out of camp at about midnight, then halted and kept in expectation of immediate departure for seven hours, then when the mid-summer sun had attained nearly its full heat, were put upon the route, and with no formal halt, but with much hesitation and frequent delay, were kept in the column fourteen weary hours.

At eleven o'clock at night, on the 15th, the Captain commanding reached the end of the day's march on the left bank of the Chickahominy, and encamped with less than thirty men, who alone had been able to keep up with the column. All night long the men came toiling in, and by the next daylight nearly all had again joined the command.

From this by easier marches, passing Williamsburg, Yorktown, and Big Bethel, we arrived August 19th at Newport News. Each day's march showed better results—officers and men gaining in health and strength as they increased their distance from Westover, and when the first breeze came to them over the salt water, the refreshing sensation was quaintly declared to be like breathing ice cream.

An amusing incident is recalled of our start from Yorktown. We broke camp at 7 A. M., 18th August. The headquarters officers' mess of our Regiment had been fortunate enough to confiscate a "muell" on the previous day; his temper proved to be not child-like nor yet bland. Upon this creature's back was loaded the kit, consisting of pots, pans, kettles, plates, etc., etc., with whatever bread, sugar, and other rations were in stock. The whole affair was in charge of a darkey. The kit was packed in two large sacks, to be hung across the mule's back, like panniers, and on top of these were piled a few bulky articles, camp-chairs, and such like nick-nacks. When fully loaded little was to be seen of "the insect," except his ears and his legs. The darkey being discouraged in the legs had made up his mind, as soon as it could be done without being seen by the officers, to mount upon the top of this pyramid of pots and pans, and to have a ride.

The mule, however, had other views. As the column filed off down the hill, rough with stumps, and ending in a morass, we looked back and saw Mr. Mule arguing and expostulating, mule-fashion, with Mr. Cuffy. At length, however, he apparently yielded to the superior forensic skill of the latter, and allowed himself to be mounted. Yet, as the sequel showed, there was a mental reservation. After wheeling round and round several times, as if to look the ground over thoroughly and examine this new question on all sides, the mule laid back his long ears, stretched his neck, and bolted straight down the hill. He stopped suddenly at the edge of the swamp, planted his fore-feet, raised his hind-quarters, and sent the other contraband-of-war some distance into the swamp, while the kettles, and coffee, etc., of the headquarters mess strewed the ground in all directions. Thereafter it was remarked that that darkey invariably led that mule; also, that several little utensils, such as cups and saucers, were missing from the table of the mess.

IV.

CAMPAIGNING UNDER POPE.

A T Newport News the Regiment immediately em-
barked on the transport steamer *Belvidere* for
Acquia Creek, thence by railroad it was forwarded
to Stafford Court House, near Fredericksburg, and
on the 22d of August encamped in a pleasant grove
not far from Barnett's Ford, on the upper Rappahannock, in which agreeable and comparatively salubri-
ous locality we enjoyed a welcome rest of several
days, but we were very hungry. Our position was
at too great distance to receive regular supplies from
Burnside at Acquia, and General Pope did not consider bases of supplies of any importance.

On Saturday, the 23d, distant firing was heard in
the direction of the upper fords of the Rappahannock. On Tuesday, the 26th, one wagon came up
for each regiment, and early on the 27th we moved
along the river, past roads leading to Kemper's and
Kelly's Fords, as far as Bealton, on the Orange and
Alexandria Railroad, then up the railroad track
towards Manassas. The sound of artillery was
often audible in advance.

This march was made through a country parched
by the heat of a Southern mid-summer, the troops

64

always enveloped in clouds of dust, the few wells and watering-places constantly in possession of a struggling crowd which barred out the weak who needed water most, and it cannot be a matter for surprise, but indeed it was a matter for grief, that hundreds of the soldiers fell exhausted by the way-side, to die in the fields, or in prison to suffer what was worse than death.

That evening we bivouacked near Warrenton Junction, in a large wood, the men as they came in throwing themselves upon the ground, hastening to get their needed sleep. The officers (who could not draw rations) felt the want of food even more than the men. The field and staff mess could offer only some wretched cakes of corn bread.

On the morning of the 28th, before many of us had fairly tasted sleep, we were aroused with orders to prepare for the march. The night was yet intensely dark and it was difficult to find the way out from the wood. The staff officers who, guided by our camp-fires, came to lead us out upon the road, a distance of three hundred yards—were obliged to acknowledge their inability to do so. At last a negro servant of the Surgeon, escorted by soldiers having lighted candles in the muzzles of their rifles, guided the Regiment and the brigade out of the wood to the roadway. Here we found the way blocked by a battery, and resort was had to torches, by whose light the men, in single file, picked their way through the obstructions. Then there was a long wait for Sykes' division, and after his files had

F

flitted by like shadows in the darkness, there came a grey daylight through the fog, by which, with great trouble we were able to move slowly on our route, winding in and out among the wagons which also had been impeded by thick darkness. At length we moved pretty rapidly in the direction of Manassas, following the line of the railway. At Catlett's a train of cars was seen which had been fired and partially destroyed; near by we passed a headquarters camp, said to have been General Pope's, which had evidently been raided by the enemy. At intervals we could hear the sound of fighting, at the north and northeast, sometimes pretty near, and we were hurried forward as rapidly as possible. At Kettle Run we saw evidences of the battle which Hooker had fought there with Ewell's corps, and saw many prisoners and wounded men. Here the fighting seemed to be northwest from us; as we crossed Broad Run, about sundown, it was nearly due north.

A day of hot sun and stifling dust was this 28th day of August; on every side were evidences that there had been heavy fighting. The railroad track had been torn up and its bridges destroyed, clearly by the rebels. The trains of wagons, the batteries, the troops of all arms that we passed or that passed us this day, were wonderful for number.

We encamped upon a large plain, a half mile beyond the Run, while the sound of artillery and musketry on our left was very distinctly heard.

At dawn next morning, Friday, August 29th, we marched toward Manassas Junction. Rapid and

fierce fighting on our left, in the direction of Bull
Run.   At the Junction, what had been a long train
of luggage cars, loaded with army equipments,
clothing, and supplies, was found a heap of smouldering ruins, and the track and bridges had been
destroyed and were yet burning.   Looking to the
north the smoke of battle could be plainly discerned.
marked by white puffs of bursting shells, and the
sound of artillery was faintly heard ; a long line of
dust extended from Thoroughfare Gap into and
apparently beyond the field of battle.

After a brief halt on the heights of Manassas, we
countermarched and took the road to Gainesville,
which here is nearly parallel to the Manassas Gap
Railroad ; we passed McDowell's corps, lying along
the roadside a mile or so from the Junction.   They
cheered and told us to "go in" and said that they
had enough of it, etc.   All this time we had had no
chance to eat or drink, and nobody seemed to
understand our movements.   The wildest rumors
were afloat ; now that Pope was cut off and captured
—now that Jackson was surrounded, pressed by
Siegel, and trying to escape by Aldie—now that
there was a large force in our rear, and that we were
cut off from Washington.   Then, and this seemed
true, that Lee or Longstreet was bringing up reinforcements to Jackson by Thoroughfare Gap, and
that Siegel, or McDowell, or Banks, or somebody
unknown, was trying to prevent this movement.

After passing McDowell's men we marched rapidly, and when five and a half or six miles out from

Manassas Junction, came to a bold elevation of
cleared land, extending from the road to the railway, and on a line nearly parallel could see a long
line of dust marking the line upon which the
enemy was moving; and when there were openings
in the wood, which for the most part masked the
moving column, we could with a good glass see
their artillery, infantry, and trains.

The cloud of dust which revealed the march of
the enemy along our front was lost on the right,
where it passed over a low wooded ridge, beyond
which was seen the battle smoke. The guns could
be heard only faintly by us in our high position, and
must have been inaudible in the woods of the valley
below.

Upon this hill we were deployed, and guns were
brought up and placed in position. Our brigade
(Griffin's) started out on the right flank, moved over
the railroad track and for some distance into the
woods, with skirmishers thrown out in the front and
on the flank, but finding no practicable way through
the woods returned and drew up on the hill. Two
or three regiments were deployed to the front as
skirmishers and sent down the hill and across the
valley, as if to feel of the enemy, whose column
continued to pour down from Thoroughfare, turning
to the northeast at a point about two miles away—
at or near Gainesville.

Generals Porter and McDowell, with other generals and their staff, stood in a group; the infantry
was closed in mass and the batteries ready for

action when, from a corn-field in the flank of the marching column in the valley, there suddenly curled a wreath of smoke, and then another and another. A round shot buried itself in the face of the hill, throwing up a cloud of dust; then one after the other two shells burst close to the general officers, killing two men of our brigade. Our own batteries promptly replied and silenced the guns in front, but they opened again further to the right with such a rake upon our infantry as to make it prudent to withdraw them to the cover of the ground. Evidently our General intended an attack, and everything was ready; but the remonstrances of Morell and Marshall prevailed upon Porter to countermand the order, and we finally bivouacked upon the hill.

On the 30th, before day-break, we took the road with orders to proceed to Centreville. Our brigade was to cover the rear in this movement, and of course was preceded in the march by the supply train of the corps. Before breakfast we had crossed Bull Run at Blackburn's Ford. It seems that orders had been sent to change the destination of our corps, but the officer charged with their delivery having followed back the column until he reached the trains, gave orders to the quartermaster in charge of them to continue on to Centreville, and either did not know or entirely forgot that our Brigade was beyond the wagons; whence it happened that while the rest of our corps was in battle on the Gainesville road, we were waiting at Centreville, wondering where they were, hearing the roar of battle as it drew nearer and nearer to our hillside, and constantly expecting orders.

At about four o'clock we started for the field of battle. Almost immediately we came upon swarms of stragglers, who had left their ranks, and who were full of stories of regiments all cut up, as well as of their individual prowess. Then came crowds of wounded men, ambulances, wagons, empty caissons, until at last the road was fairly blocked with officers and men in no order, horses, wagons, and batteries. Men were running, panting, cursing, and some worn out and exhausted had thrown themselves upon the ground by the roadside utterly indifferent to their fate; and now we knew that this was the route of an exhausted army, and that our duty was to guard their rear.

Forcing our way through all, just as we came to the well-ordered but retreating lines, night came on; and although there were yet sounds of desultory firing, and occasional shot or shells plunging and exploding about us, the fight was over, and in the gloom of night we marched slowly back with the throng of troops to the heights of Centreville.

Next morning, Sunday, August 31st, 1862, it was raining hard. The scene of confusion about us beggars description, and everybody was hungry, wet, and dispirited. Before noon, however, order began to come out of chaos. Men found their colors, and regiments and brigades their appointed stations, and our Brigade moved out upon the Gainesville Pike to receive the first onset of the enemy.

Our position was on the right of the turnpike, and the line extended north and east toward Fairfax, with a strong picket two or three hundred yards in front, and here we passed the afternoon in quiet.

All day Monday, September 1st, trains of ambulances, under flags of truce, were going out to the field of battle and returning loaded with wounded men. The weather continued cold and rainy, with a northeast wind. Toward evening the sound of fighting was heard in the direction of Chantilly. The men were wet to the skin, rations exhausted, no fires allowed. Surgeons coming in from the battle-field reported the enemy in great force a very short distance out on the turnpike, and on the old Warrenton Road, waiting the order to attack. The night was passed in misery; the hazard of our position forbade sleep, and comfort was impossible. The army had moved from Centreville, in our rear, and at 3 A. M. we drew in our pickets and moved quietly away.

Looking back as we left Centreville, we saw the enemy coming into the town in great numbers, but they made no attack. At Fairfax Court House we met large bodies of troops; thence, taking a northeast course, we passed Vienna, and toward evening struck the Leesburg Turnpike. Beyond Levinsville we were met by General McClellan, who was enthusiastically greeted by the troops, and at 11 P. M. we bivoucked at Langley's, after a march of twenty-eight miles.

Wednesday, September 3d, we encamped on Miners Hill, near Falls Church, which was the

locality of Porter's command previous to the Peninsula campaign.

Our active campaign with the army of Virginia
comprised only ten days as almanacs count time,
but these were days so full of excitement and of
incident that memory recalls a whirl of occurences
and events, succeeding so rapidly one to another
that it is with difficulty one can separate them.
There are pictures, but they are changing with the
rapidity of those of the kaleidoscope.

One scene constantly recurring, not only on this,
but on many another march, presents to us again the
array of sick or exhausted men, who strewed the
route of the hurried columns—their pinched and
worn faces—their eyes half closed, gazing into
space—their bodies crouched or cramped with pain,
supported against trees or fences, or lying prone
upon the ground; the men almost always clinging to
their rifles. "If one had told me yesterday," said
an officer on his first march with the army, "that
I could pass one man so stricken, and not stop
to aid or console him, I should have resented the
charge as a slander, and already I have passed
hundreds." Many, many such, necessarily abandoned to their fate, crept into the woods and died.
Under repeated orders, all men absent and not
accounted for, should have been reported as deserters, but Captains were more merciful than the
orders, and few were found to brand as ignominious
the names of men who deserved rather to be canon-
ized as martyrs.

Another memory is of a gallant Captain of artillery, whose battery marched just in advance of our Regiment—of an aide galloping back and wheeling to the Captain's side to communicate an order—the quick question, "where?" a short answer, a note of a bugle, and the Captain dashes off to our left, followed by his battery—the thunderous rumble of caissons and gun-carriages dying away as they pass out of our sight over a swell of land. It is strange that as this scene is recalled where a fellow-soldier rushed to immediate death, a prominent feature of the picture is the vivid color of the mass of blue flowers which clothed the entire field through which his battery dashed away from our column.

Another turn of the mnemonic glass, and we see the country about Manassas trodden into a vast highway. Just there Stuart had captured a train laden with quartermaster's stores, and the ground all about was strewn with broken cases and what had been their contents—new uniforms, underclothing, hats and shoes, from which men helped themselves at will, leaving the old where they found the new. Near by, on the railroad track, waited a long train loaded with sick and wounded—the cars packed full, and many lying on the top unsheltered in the sun.

Yet again, and we are in sight of Thoroughfare, and see the long lines of dust revealing the march of Lee's army down towards us from the Gap, and we remember the applause we gave when the first shell from Hazlitt's parrot guns exploded exactly in a line of rebel infantry (scattering them as is rarely done except in cheap engravings), and how little we appreciated the like accuracy of aim by which an enemy's shot killed two men in one of our own regiments.

And again there comes a mental photograph, date and locality indistinct, which represents nineteen officers gathered about a sumptuous repast, comprising three loaves of old bread, a fragment of cheese and a half canteen of water, almost as stale as the bread, and the careful watch of Field upon Staff and Staff upon Line, to see that only one swallow of water is taken by each in his turn.

And finally, we stand blocking the way to gaze upon a wrecked omnibus, inscribed—"Georgetown and Navy Yard"—one of many vehicles impressed in Washington and sent out as ambulances, and which, after reviving in us memories of civilization, was to become a trophy in the hands of the enemy.

V.

OUR THIRD BATTALION.

WHEN the 32d Regiment left Massachusetts in May, the war fever was raging, and it was supposed that it would be the work but of a few days to recruit the four companies required to complete the Regiment, and it was clearly understood that the first recruits were to be assigned to us. But being out of sight we were indeed out of mind, and the pressure of officers interested in constructing new regiments constantly delayed our claims to consideration.

In two months over three thousand volunteers had been accepted, of whom only one hundred (our Company G) had been assigned to us. The rendezvous for the Eastern part of the State was the camp at Lynnfield, which was placed under the command of Colonel Maggi, of the 33d. His own regiment occupied the chief part of the camp, and the only entrance to it was through his regimental guard. Both he and his Lieutenant Colonel, a young and handsome officer named Underwood, had a quick eye for a promising recruit, and as the constantly arriving volunteers passed within the lines, the best were drafted into the 33d, and the remainder were passed into the command of Major Wilde, whose camp was just beyond.

Dr. Edward A. Wilde, afterward Colonel of the 35th Massachusetts, and yet later Brigadier General of Volunteers, was commissioned, July 24th, 1862, to fill the the then vacant majority in the 32d, and had been temporarily placed in charge of the unattached volunteers at Lynnfield, three hundred of whom had been roughly fashioned into companies, and were to be assigned to us.

Upon Colonel Parker's return to Massachusetts, Governor Andrew gave to our matters his willing attention. Upon inspection of the three companies, the Colonel thought that he could do better than to take Colonel Maggi's rejected recruits, and they were accordingly transferred to the 35th.

At the urgent request of the authorities of Newton, supported by the Honorable J. Wiley Edmands, a company raised entirely in that town was regimented in the 32d. A company from Charlestown was made the basis of Company I, and taking a lesson from Colonel Maggi, whose regiment happily was now filled, a third company was organized at the camp by selecting from the town quotas the choicest material, and passing over the remainder to the 35th. We were able to accomplish this by the active aid of our Major Wilde. If the Major had known that he was to be the first Colonel of the 35th, that regiment might perhaps have been benefitted, but the 32d undoubtedly owed to his want of prophetic vision the fact that its 3d Battalion was composed of men in every respect equal to those of its First.

On the 2d of August the companies were detached from Major Wilde's recruits and ordered to report to Colonel Parker, who at once moved them some eight hundred yards away, where they encamped in a charming spot, between the pond and the highway, until they should be provided with clothing, arms, and equipments.

The beauty and convenience of that camp has impressed its memory upon every soldier of the Battalion; but the proprietor of the land did not seem to be equally pleased with an arrangement to which very possibly his previous consent was not obtained; but if he expected to drive us away by removing the rope and bucket from the well near by, he was sadly disappointed. He presented to the Colonel a huge bill for the use of the premises, and for damages caused by the cutting down of a sapling elm, and the removal of a rod or two of stone wall. If he never collected it he should have been comforted by the fact that we never charged him for the construction of two good wells on the ground, and the stones of his fence may yet be found in the walls of those wells.

On the 6th Colonel Parker left to rejoin the regiment, leaving the Battalion to follow under Major Wilde, but the Major was promoted to the 35th, and it was not until the 20th that the three companies, commanded by the senior Captain (Moulton), left

Lynnfield by railroad to Somerville, thence marching to Charlestown, where a generous entertainment had been provided for them by the citizens. That even- 'ing they left by the Providence Railroad—the entire route through the cities of Charlestown and Boston being one ovation. At Stonington they took the steamer, landing the next morning at Jersey City, and taking a train for Philadelphia. Through that good city they marched to the Cooper Refreshment Rooms, and being well fed and otherwise refreshed, moved thence to the Baltimore Station. It was well into the next day before they arrived in that town of doubtful loyalty, and it was morning on the 22d when they landed in Washington, and took up quarters at the railroad barracks.

While the commanding officer was endeavoring to find somebody to give him orders, several hours of liberty were allowed to the men, few of whom had ever seen Washington. It was not the quiet place that it had been when the right wing arrived there months before, but was again astir with signs of active war. The movement to effect a junction between the armies of Generals McClellan and Pope was in progress, and long trains of wagons were moving between Alexandria and the various depots of supplies, and ambulances loaded with sick and wounded streamed to and from the hospitals, while on the walks, men in uniforms, some brand new and some ragged and dirty, jostled each other; new recruits from the North—garrison men from the forts—stragglers and convalescents from the armies in the field.

If at the word hospital there is presented to the mind's eye of the reader a spacious structure in stone or brick, covered with a dome and expanding into wings, all embosomed in a park-like enclosure, with verdant lawns shaded by trees and mottled with shrubbery, that reader did not go to muster in Virginia in '62. Provision thought to be ample had been made in Washington, by the construction in several unoccupied squares, of rows of detached wooden sheds, each of which was the ward of a · hospital. Rough and unattractive as these appeared set down among the dusty streets, upon a plot of land from which every green thing was trodden out, their interiors were in fact models of neatness, and in some sort, of comfort. But the battles of the Peninsula had soon filled these, and when there were added to them the sick from McClellan's army and the invalids from Pope's, every available building was taken, and finally when within ten days, eight thousand patients were added from the James River, vacant house-lots were occupied, and for want of tents, awnings of sails or boards were laid over rough frames, and the passer-by could see the patients stretched upon the straw. The happy result of this, and other enforced experiments, was to prove that even these wretched makeshifts were better than close-walled houses, for hospital purposes.

On the 23d the Battalion marched over Long Bridge to the town of Alexandria—preferring at night the outside of the building designated to shelter them. The next day tents and wagons were obtained, and on the 25th their first camp was made on the hillside, near the Seminary.

Everything in that neighborhood was in confusion. During the week that the command remained encamped, Franklin's and Sumner's corps arrived at Alexandria, and not only was the town crowded with soldiers, but the woods were full of them, and all the energies of the authorities were devoted to endeavors to supply them, and push them out to the rescue of General Pope's army.

Considering that nobody, not even the General-in-chief, knew where Pope's army was, it is not surprising that all the efforts made by officers to find our Regiment were fruitless; indeed it mattered little that they were, for the wagons were taken away for the pressing service of more experienced troops, who were unable to move for want of transportation.

At last, on the 3d of September, the locality of Porter's Corps was ascertained, and the Battalion joined the rest of the Regiment. There was a striking contrast in the appearance of the old and new companies. The three new companies outnumbered all the other seven. The veterans looked with wonder upon the fresh northern faces and the bright new uniforms, while the recruits scanned with at least equal surprise the mud-stained, worn, and weary men who were to be their comrades. So long were the new platoons, that the detachment was christened "Moulton's Brigade," but the superiority of numbers was not long with them, and two weeks of campaigning amalgamated the command.

The three companies comprising our "3d Battalion" were —

Company H, recruited at the Lynnfield Camp, commanded by Captain Henry W. Moulton; its Lieutenants were John H. Whidden and Joseph W. Wheelwright.

Company I, recruited in Charlestown, Captain Hannibal D. Norton; Lieutenants, Chas. H. Hurd and Lucius H. Warren, since Brevet Brigadier-General.

Company K, recruited in Newton, Captain J. Cushing Edmands, afterwards Colonel and Brevet Brigadier-General; Lieutenants, Ambrose Bancroft and John F. Boyd.

At Upton's Hill the complete organization of the Regiment was published in the orders. The Lieutenant Colonel was promoted to be Colonel, Captain Prescott to be Lieutenant Colonel, and Captain Stephenson to be Major. The medical staff consisted of Z. Boylston Adams, Surgeon, with the rank of Major; William Lyman Faxon and W. H. Bigelow, Assistant Surgeons, ranking as First Lieutenants; W. T. M. Odiorne, Hospital Steward. The non-commissioned staff consisted of James P. Wade, Sergeant Major; James A. White, Quartermaster Sergeant; Charles E. Madden, Commissary Sergeant; and Freeman Field, Principal Musician.

Dr. Bigelow, Steward Odiorne, and Sergeant Madden, were new appointments. All the rest had

6

been with the Regiment through all its experience in the field.

No chaplain was ever commissioned in the 32d, no application having ever been made on the part of the line officers, to whom belonged the initiative, and none being desired, so far as was known by any officer or man.

In an army composed of men of many different religious beliefs, as was the case in ours, the chaplains should constitute a staff corps, its members proportioned as to faith, in some degree to the requirements of the army, so that from the headquarters of an army or corps details might be made of the proper men for any required duty. Attached to regimental headquarters, they were very generally utterly inefficient for good professionally. It was the rule with us that, when any of the sick were near death, the fact should be reported to the commanding officer, who was often the first to communicate the tidings, and who invariably enquired of the dying man if he desired the service of a chaplain. When this was desired, an orderly was sent with the compliments of the Colonel, to some chaplain near by, to ask his attendance. With only rare exceptions such services were cheerfully and promptly rendered.

The burial service was usually read by the commanding officer over the bodies of our dead; but in one case, where the man had been a Roman Catholic, it was thought better to ask the attendance of a chaplain of that faith. It happened that the orderly could not readily find one, and could find only one, and returned with the unusual reply that the chaplain could not come.

Upon further inquiry it appeared that the orderly had presented the message, with the compliments of the Colonel, to the chaplain, who was reposing after dinner. "Was he a good Catholic?" enquired the priest. The orderly assured him that he was. "My compliments to the Colonel, then, and tell him he can bury him. It is all right." With which reply the messenger was compelled to return. Failing the orderly's assurance of the man's good and regular standing, of course the chaplain would have escaped the duty too.

In November, 1862, our camp hospital offered merely a canvas tent for shelter, and some straw spread upon the frosty ground for bedding. One of the patients, in view of approaching death, expressed to the Adjutant his wish to be baptized, and of course a messenger was sent forth to seek a chaplain, with the customary compliments, and to ask his attendance on a dying man.

A chaplain promptly appeared at our headquarters, was escorted to the hospital tent and left at the side of the sick man. Very soon after, the Colonel, meeting the reverend officer pacing thoughtfully in the open air, stopped and enquired as to the patient's condition. Evidently considerably embarrassed, the chaplain said "you did not tell me that the man wanted baptism." "Very true," was the reply, "but why is that any difficulty?" "Because," rejoined the

clergyman, hesitatingly, "I am of the Baptist per-
suasion, and this is no case for immersion."

It was very awkward, but the Colonel, who had
thought only of a chaplain as the proper officer for
a present duty, apologized for his want of thought,
thanked the gentleman, and said that he would try
again, or if it became necessary, would himself ad-
minister the holy rite. The chaplain, however, requested a few minutes for reflection, at the end of
which he decided to officiate himself and did so, first
taking the precaution to enquire of the soldier
whether he preferred immersion or sprinkling, the
latter of which very naturally was elected.

VI.

THE ANTIETAM CAMPAIGN.

Until September 12th, our Division remained at Upton's Hill, while the rest of the Army of the Potomac drew off into Maryland in observation of General Lee, concerning whose movements no definite information could for a time be obtained.

It was a favorite theory among the authorities in Washington that General Lee would lead McClellan off into Western Maryland, and then slip round into his rear and capture the aforesaid authorities. Of course 80,000 men do not slip about such a country very easily, and of course General Lee would never have dared to place his army between the forts of Washington and the Army of the Potomac; but even such absurd fears required consideration, and in addition to the artillery garrisons in the forts and the new levies inside the defences, Morell's division was left for a time to watch the approaches to the Chain Bridge, which was the weakest point in the defences of the city.

During these days the various corps of the army whose organization a week before had been almost destroyed, were marching through the town. in columns of platoons, with their drums beating and colors flying, their array as fine as it would have been on parade before they had ever seen the enemy, and inspiring all who saw them to a happy augury of the result of the first Maryland campaign.

On the 11th, our Division received orders to join the army in the field with all possible speed, and on the 12th we folded our tents, and took the route in the track of our comrades. As usual the start was delayed until the sun was well up in the sky, and before we were out of the District of Columbia the heat had become oppressive, and the men, especially those of the new companies, were suffering greatly. Our route was from Upton's Hill past Fort Corcoran, through Georgetown and Washington, and out by 7th street.

Early in the day came a circular order to be read at the head of each company denouncing the penalty of death, without trial, as the punishment for straggling, the utter absurdity of which was shown by the fact that before nightfall one-third of the men had fallen out of their ranks, the order to the contrary notwithstanding. The old soldiers, happily, (or unhappily) had learned that the bark of the orders was worse than their bite, but the new recruits had the impression, as yet, that orders meant what they said, and believed that the officers would shoot down all those who faltered; consequently, what between soldierly ambition and personal fear, the new men would struggle on until they could do so no longer. The day was burning hot, and the last hour before noon was chosen to give the command one pull of three miles without rest; and when at last the bugle sounded "halt," not less than fifty of our men fell exhausted, fainting or sunstruck, several of them raving with insane imaginings.

Although we tarried at this place for an hour or more, the Colonel assuming the responsibility to fall out with his entire command, it was found necessary at last to leave some twenty men who needed rest and care, the greater part of whom were finally discharged from hospitals disabled for service. Here, too, in order to lighten the march, a quantity of knapsacks and blankets were left stored in a barn, but before our teams could return for them the whole had been gobbled by stragglers.

It was after dark when at last we halted for the night, and the Adjutant's returns showed that one of the new companies then numbered three officers and seven men, and another no officers and one man* present for duty. We bivouacked in columns of companies, and that one man executed under his own command the company right wheel, dressed his ranks, stacked his arm (by plunging the bayonet into the ground), called the roll, broke ranks, supped, and slept the sleep of the just.

The next two days' march brought us, via Middlebrook, Clarksville, and Hyattstown to Frederick; the weather, though clear, was not so hot as on the 12th, the men were in better condition and, on the whole, we gained in numbers. Many will remem-

---

* Private Isaac W. Thurlow, of Methuen, afterward promoted to be Lieutenant C. T.

ber our bivouac that Sunday evening as the place where they indulged in a welcome bath in the clear waters of the Monocacy river.   All day on the 14th (Sunday), we heard heavy firing, and on the 15th the sound of heavy guns at Harper's Ferry continued to assure us that our flag still was there, but its sudden cessation at last told as plainly of the surrender.

Our march of the 15th and 16th, although rapid, was not exhausting; the air was more autumnal, and we were cheered by the evidence of the fact that we were the pursuers.   Large numbers of rebel prisoners passed us going to our rear.   As we marched through Frederick we were greeted with hearty cheers from civilians and the waving kerchiefs of ladies, and children distributed ripe fruits, which were most welcome to the bilious soldiers.   On the South Mountain battle-field a detail was burying the dead, and we saw many bodies in grey uniforms awaiting burial.   We had previously met and saluted the dead General Reno, borne to the rear in an ambulance draped with the national colors.

As we passed over one of the mountain ridges, there broke upon our sight a view such as New England cannot offer.   A valley stretching far away on either hand, everywhere divided into large fields of rich farming lands, among which the homes of well-to-do farmers stood, with groups of barns and granges and hay ricks gathered about them, the whole testifying to the comfort and wealth of the inhabitants.   At every house there were words of

welcome and cheer. The entire population evidently was in sympathy with our cause, and their
recent sight of the retreating army of the enemy
had evidently strengthened their enthusiasm for his
pursuers.

It was almost sundown on the 16th when we came
up with main body of our army between Keedys-
ville and Antietam Creek. The air was full of
smoke from the camp-fires, and the hillsides alive
with the men, who were making ready for their
supper and their sleep. Our Division was guided
into the field assigned to us, and our men were soon
deep in similar preparations.

We knew that the hostile armies were now face
to face, and that a great battle was imminent.
Curiosity led many to gather on the hilltops and to
look over what was to be the battlefield, to the crests
of the low hills on the opposite bank of the stream,
where we could see the spires of the little town of
Sharpsburg sharply defined against the warm sky,
and the smoke from the rebel camp-fires glowing in
the light of the setting sun. A few well-directed
shells from the enemy's batteries however, dulled
our curiosity in that direction, and we turned to our
camps to see how an army looks upon the eve of a
pitched battle.

The eastward slopes of the hills on the left branch
of the Antietam were occupied by the infantry
of the army of McClellan, extending some four
miles from right to left. Near the tops of these hills
a few batteries of artillery were ready for use at a

moment's notice, but more of them were below us, their horses feeding at the picket ropes, the men busy about their supper.

Farther away to the rear the ammunition wagons were parked, those of each division by themselves, and yet farther back the supply trains of the different corps, and the reserve divisions of artillery and cavalry.

There was every show of complete readiness for the morrow, in the array of the troops and the provision for the fight—but everything was busy and cheery. As night fell the smoke became less dense, and the bright light of a thousand glowing fires enlivened the scene. There was no sign of haste or of anxiety; occasionally a mule sounded his trumpet as a signal for more feed, and often the sound of horses' feet was heard as some officer or orderly galloped leisurely by; there was some singing and much laughter heard from the various camps, and at last the stirring but confused sound of the tattoo along the whole line from the bugles of the distant cavalry and the neighboring artillery, and the drums and fifes of the infantry of the line.

Then came gentle sleep, nowhere more grateful and welcome than in the bivouac of the soldier on the night before the battle.

From dawn to dark no fairer sky was ever seen than that beneath which, on the 17th day of September, 1862, was fought the battle of the Antietam. It may be doubted whether there was in the history of our civil war, any instance of a battle for which the preparation was on both sides so complete, of which the field was more free and open to the movements of the troops and the oversight of the commanders, or in which the result depended so directly upon the ability of the generals and the conduct of the troops, and so little upon purely accidental occurrences.

The Confederate army occupied the crest of the rising ground which lies immediately west of the Antietam, and between it and the Potomac. That portion of this crest in which lay the left and the centre of their army, was for the most part wooded and broken by outcropping ledges, and through it ran roads whose fences and cuts afforded frequent vantage ground for a defensive force. Their right was in an open country, but one intersected by stone walls, and presenting on the side toward the Union lines very abrupt declivities.

The left of our army (directly opposite the rebel right), were posted on low hills, whose western sides were also steep and rough. Between the two positions the gap was just sufficient for the passage of the little river and for a narrow country road on either bank, and here the stream was spanned by a stone bridge of three arches, since known as Burnside's bridge.

Nearly a mile above, over a similar bridge, the Sharpsburg turnpike crossed the Antietam, cutting by a direct line the centres of both armies. Lying across this road, east of the river, on commanding ground, the corps of Gen. Porter held the centre of the loyal army, connecting with Burnside on the left and with Sumner on the right. On the right of the Union army was Hooker's corps, on the west bank of the stream, and almost in contact with the rebel left, occupying the ground which they had won from the enemy at nightfall of the day before; both parties in the same wood sleeping on their arms in line of battle.

Taken together, the positions of the two armies described a figure not unlike the letter D, of which the curved portion may represent the Union lines, and the straight part (which was in fact also curved), those of the Confederates. Except at our left (the bottom of the D), our army held both banks of the Antietam, and at both extremes the two armies almost touched.

Standing among the guns of Porter's batteries, about the centre of the Union lines, one seemed to look down upon the field, the whole of which, except the immediate vicinity of Burnside's bridge, was open to the view. Directly in our front the Antietam washed the base of the hill, on the rounded summit of which the guns were placed, but from the farther bank the land rose gently rolling to the lines of the army of our enemy. Between us and the rebel centre were cleared fields, many of them bearing crops of nearly ripened corn, bounded to the left by steep hill-sides closing in to the river, but on the right running up to a glade bordered by woodlands. In these woods, and in and over that glade, occurred the severest struggles and the great-

est slaughter of this hard-fought battle. Near
Porter's lines, on yet higher land, the headquarters
of our army were established for the day.

Of the curving line of the union army, the left
was the corps of General Burnside, the centre the
corps of General Porter, and the right the corps of
General Hooker ; but in the rear of Hooker was the
corps of General Mansfield, and behind it that of
General Sumner, while the force of General Franklin, just up from Pleasant Valley, acted as the
reserve.

McClellan's plan of the battle was to make the
principal attack from his right, but as soon as that
was well engaged, to throw Burnside from his left
against the right of Lee, not absolutely as a real
attack, but by menacing the road to the ford which
was Lee's only line of retreat, to occupy and divert
certain portions of the Confederate army, and thus
reduce its power of resistance to the real attack
upon the other flank.

By reason of the curvation of the line, our batteries in its centre could reach effectively the whole
extent of the front of the enemy from left to right ;
and throughout the day, as opportunity offered, the
guns did good execution, and more especially upon
our right where we could annoy the rebel infantry
while in the cover of the woods, and enfilade them
whenever they appeared in the open glade.

At break of day the rattling volleys of musketry
on the right told that Hooker was opening the great
struggle. Soon occasional deep thuds of his cannon

were also heard, then nearer and more constant came
the sounds approaching from both wings, until our
own batteries in the centre joined in the din.   Along
the whole line gun for gun came back—as if echoed
from the other ridge—the voice of the invading army
from lips of bronze and iron, and its exploding mes-
sengers repeated in our ears the arguments of war,
until hundreds of heavy guns were united in one
deep quivering roar.   And although there was rising and falling in the sound, yet until nightfall the
sound of battle never ceased.

Just across the creek the skirmishers of our corps
showed like dotted lines upon the fields; now and
then we could see the smoke puff from their rifles,
although the sound was lost in that of the general
conflict.   On the left, until afternoon, no movements
were visible, but across that open glade, far away on
the right, the tide of battle ebbed and flowed.

First from the edge of the woods on our side,
appeared a ragged line of men fleeing for their
lives, and following them the solid front of Hooker's corps, firing as it followed.

The fugitives were three brigades of Jackson's
men, and the dark spots before the advancing line
were the first fruits of that harvest of slaughter, whose
winrows before nightfall traversed the whole of that
fatal glade.

Hooker's men had nearly crossed the open ground
when the whole of Jackson's corps burst from the
western wood and met them in the open field;
Hooker against Jackson—that was the tug of war.

No sign of yielding could be marked on either side. Both lines became involved in the smoke of their rifles, but whenever the breeze wafted the smoke away, the reduced number of the combatants could be noted, and the fringe of wounded men and their too numerous helpers, which always hangs from the rear in the battle line, was constantly visible between each body and its nearest sheltering wood.

There was no moment when this contest ended; no line was seen pursuing or pursued, but little by little both melted away; and when all were gone, out from the edge of the woods on either side belched the fire and smoke of the batteries.

Now seven o'clock by Sharpsburg time. The scattered men of the broken divisions of each army sought the friendly shelter of the lines which were advancing to relieve them. Hood of Longstreet's command, was marshalling his brigades within the timber on the west, and Mansfield's corps was moving up through the rough woodland on the east, and for a season the open space between was unoccupied save by the dead and wounded, and the rolling, drifting smoke from the artillery.

The next movement visible to us was from the Confederate side, whence, with a rapid rush, came the command of General Hood,—Texas, Georgia, and Alabama men. In a few minutes they had crossed the open field in the face of our guns, and although a portion of their line faltered, yet another pushed even up to the line of our batteries, silencing almost every gun. Mansfield had fallen, but his men were there, and their rattling volleys showed that the enemy could get no foothold in the wood, just in the edge of which the line of smoke hung steadily an hour or more.

At nine o'clock the contest was for the moment ended by the advance of Sedgwick's division of Sumner's corps, before which the southern troops broke and fled over the glade to the cover opposite, and again our guns opened upon their shelter.

Sedgwick's division was the right of Sumner's corps, and now between it and us moved up from the Antietam the divisions of Richardson and French, his left and centre. Unobserved by the enemy, we could see them forming for the attack, and we watched with intense interest their steady progress diagonally across our front. As they crossed the summit of each rise, they came under the fire of the rebel batteries; but our twenty-pounders playing over their heads, kept the rebel lines crackling with shells, to the comfort of our friends and the confusion of their foes. In each depression of the land Richardson and French halted to dress their ranks, and then moved quickly on; and so they won closer and closer to the enemy, until they were so near that the guns of our batteries could not help nor those of the enemy hurt them. Here, in a field of standing corn, they came upon the infantry of General Hill, who, protected by fences and road cuttings, opened a galling fire. Receiving but not answering this, Sumner's divisions, aided by horse batteries from Porter's

corps, dashed forward and secured these defences
for themselves, driving out the Confederate infantry
on the right, capturing or slaying them in the
sunken road on the left. For a few brief minutes
the carnage was terrific.

Here Richardson and French, not without frequent contests, held their advanced position all the
day. We have described their movement as if it
had been an isolated one; but it was not so. The
right of Sumner's corps, the division of "Old John"
Sedgwick, was carrying everything before it. It
swept in solid form across the glade, and pushed
out of our sight into and through what we have
called the western wood, and into the open land
beyond.

The violence of this attack outran discretion and
the division found itself out in the open fields with
no support on either flank, and met by fresh troops
of the enemy. Falling slowly back it came into
line with the division of General French, but leaving a great gap between, into which the advancing
forces of the enemy hastened to drive a cleaving
wedge.

It was now one o'clock P. M., and we held the
whole of the right and centre of General Lee's original position, but not firmly. Besides the danger at
the gap between Sedgwick and French, the latter
was short of ammunition and Sedgwick's right was
feeble.

At this time, most opportunely, McClellan ordered forward his reserve, the corps of General

H

Franklin; and that officer dividing his command, closed up the threatened gap, re-inforced French's line and strengthened Sedgwick's right, welding the whole to such tough consistency that no further impression could be made. What we had won we held.

Three o'clock in the afternoon and nothing seen of Burnside yet.

The most untutored of those who had watched the varying fortunes of the field could see that if Lee's right had been attacked while McClellan was thus hammering on his left, either his right or left must have yielded. We had seen troops moving from the one flank to reinforce the other, until it seemed as if none could remain to hold the right. From officers about the headquarters we knew that McClellan, in person, had the night before advanced the division of Burnside's corps close to the bridge, and that he had told that general to reconnoitre carefully, in readiness for attacking in the morning. We knew that at six o'clock he had been ordered to form his troops for the assault upon the bridge, and that at eight o'clock orders had been sent to carry the bridge, gain the heights, and move upon Sharpsburg.

General McClellan himself looked not more anxiously for movement on the left, than did we who saw the gallant fighting of the right; but five hours had passed before the capture of the bridge by the twin 51sts of New York and Pennsylvania, and since then two more of those priceless hours had passed away. Oh! if Sheridan or our Griffin could but have been commanding there.

The last peremptory order to advance and "not to stop for loss of life" produced the wished-for movement, but it was too late and too hesitating to accomplish great results.

When, at last, the heights were gained, the division of A. P. Hill had arrived to reinforce the enemy, who could also spare something from in front of our now-weakened right.

Burnside's men fought well — gave only slowly back, and that not far. Six battalions of regulars from our corps moved to the front, joining the right of Burnside's corps to the left of Sumner's, and leaving our (Morell's) division, in the rear of the advanced line, the only reserve force of McClellan's army. One brigade was sent to the left to strengthen Burnside, and at five P. M., our own, the last, was marched toward the right, but the declining sun already showed that the contest for the day must soon be ended. Just as it reached the horizon there was one roaring *feu d'enfer* along both lines, and almost of a sudden the firing ceased, and the battle of the Antietam had filled its page in history. It was an important victory. By it Washington, Maryland, and Pennsylvania were relieved from menace and the country for a time was grateful.

Just as it appeared to the looker-on the battle of Antietam has been described. What happened, before our eyes has been told, without digressions, and the digressions may now be added.

The battle-field was all day long bathed in sunshine; hardly one cloud appeared to throw even a
passing shadow over the fair autumnal landscape, of
which the background was made up of shadowed
tracts of woodland, and into which were introduced
blocks of rough pasture, lawn-like vistas, rolling
fields of corn ready for the harvest, with just enough
of distant spire and nearer farmstead to add a look
of human comfort to the natural beauty of the scene.
Although the foreground and the middle distance of
this picture were occupied by the various combatants
— killing and maiming — wounded and dying —
there was present to our sight no blemish of horror.
We saw no ghastly wounds, no streams of flowing
gore; we heard no groans nor sighs nor oaths of
the struggle, and rarely did the sound even of southern yells or northern cheers penetrate the massive
roar of ordnance to reach our ears; and yet before
our eyes was fought a battle in which four thousand
men were slain, and fifteen thousand more were disabled by savage wounds.

So entirely were the sadder sights of bloody war
excluded from our minds, that when two men of our
Regiment were badly wounded by the accidental discharge of a falling rifle, the incident created almost
as much excitement as one like it might have done
at a muster of militia here at home.

It must not be imagined that any one of us stood
throughout that equinoctial day gazing upon the
sunlit scene beyond the Antietam, for in time even
the terrible events of battle fall tamely upon eye and

ear. In the long pauses between the rounds of infantry fighting we sat down upon the green sward and ate our lunch, or strolled away to talk with the staff officers about the headquarters, or over to one of our other brigades to discuss the incidents of the action, or to hear or tell the news of its latest casualties.

The rank and file who had not the same liberty to stray away, and who, screened from the field by the knoll on which our batteries were planted, saw little or nothing of the fight — passed the time in chat with laugh and story, as they stood, or sat, or laid, keeping in some sort the form of the massed column which was more distinctly marked by lines of rifles in the stack. Every man of them knew that at any moment he might be called to be reaper or grain in the harvest of death so near at hand; but men cannot keep themselves strained up to the pitch of heroic thought or wearing anxiety, and so within the line of battle our men joked and laughed and talked and ate, or even slept in the warm sunshine.

No heartier laugh ever rewarded Irish wit than that which shook our sides when Guiney, the handsome Colonel of the Massachusetts 9th, bedecking himself in the gorgeous apparel of a brilliant sash, was reminded that it would make him a capital mark for the enemy's sharp-shooters, and replied, "and wouldn't you have me a handsome corpse?"

Early in the day, as soon as we were in position in rear of the batteries, some of our mounted officers naturally desiring to get a correct idea of the lay of

the land and the order of the battle, rode at a foot
pace to the summit of the knoll in front, and from their
saddles were quietly examining the position of
affairs through field-glasses, and pointing hither and
yon as they conversed, when the chief of some rebel
battery, possibly suspecting them to be big generals
and high functionaries, began from two guns some
practice with round shot, using the mounted officers
for the bull's-eye of the target. In their innocence
they assumed that this sort of thing was a matter of
course on such occasions, and for a time they went
on with their observations.

It was not long however before the aim became
more accurate, and our officers suddenly became
aware of the scared looks of the German gunners,
who, watching for the smoke of the rebel guns,
dodged behind the trail of their own pieces until the
shot had passed by, and presently a sergeant ventured to suggest that the gentlemen were drawing
the fire on the battery, and to prefer the request
that they would send away the horses and pursue
their study of the field dismounted, which not
unwillingly they did.

Not far from mid-day, in an interval of comparative quiet along the lines, most of us stretched at
full length basking in the sun and waiting for "what
next?" enjoyed a beautiful sight in the endeavor of
the enemy to shell our division.

As we were hidden from his view no direct shot
could reach us, and he seemed to have calculated
that by exploding his shells high in the air, the frag-

ments could be dropped among our ranks. What became of the fragments we did not know, hardly one of them fell near us, none of them did us injury ; but we watched for the shells with interest, and were sorry when they came no more. Gazing up into the clear blue sky there would from time to time suddenly appear a little cloudlet, which unfolding itself drifted lazily away, and soon melted in the air. Each of these cloudlets was the smoke from an exploding shell, the rapid flight of which gave no other evidence of its existence to the eye, and all sound was lost in the general tumult. Each seemingly miraculous appearance of the cloudlet was hailed with admiration, and we were quite ready to enjoy the entertainment as long as our friend the enemy chose to supply it, and were inclined to be gruff with him when it stopped.

While the divisions of Generals Richardson and French were advancing on the Confederate centre, a gun from one of Porter's horse batteries was run out quite a distance to the left, where, from a little swell of land, entirely unsupported, it opened upon the rebel infantry. The rake upon the enemy's line was so complete that after the first few shots we could see them breaking ; but the position was untenable and after the gun had been discharged perhaps a dozen times, the enemy got two guns to bear upon it, whereupon our gun was hastily limbered up and went scampering back to cover as fast as four horses could run with it, and as it went rebel shots could be seen striking up the dust all about its track, as the stones strike about an escaping dog when boys are pelting him.

When such an incident occurred we could hardly refrain from cheers. And when—as was once or twice the case—we could see some movement of the enemy against our lines which was unseen to those it menaced, it was almost irresistible to cry out a warning, and several times shells from the batteries of our division gave to the Union troops the first warning of a threatening movement.

Twenty-five days after the battle our Company C on detached service encamped for a night on the plateau, the summit of the heights which were won by Burnside's charge, and Captain Fuller observing that the line of battle could even then be traced by the cartridge papers which lay in winrows on the ground, wondered that troops which had so gallantly charged up the steep ascent should have halted in this place long enough to have used so many cartridges.

On the 18th of September, Porter's corps relieved Burnside's at the lower bridge, and then we saw only too many of the woful sights which belong to battle, and saw them without that halo of excitement which in the midst of the contest diminishes their horror.

On the 19th, at dawn, we were in expectation of immediate participation in a second battle, but the enemy had retreated. In the pursuit Porter led the way. After passing through the town of Sharpsburg, the artillery occupied the roadway, the infantry moving along the fields on either side. At each rise of the land, a few pieces dashed to the summit and shelled the nearer woods, the infantry forming in the hollow in the rear, and so we felt our way a mile or two down to the Potomac. The rear guard of the enemy had just crossed the river, and General Griffin with parts of two brigades followed closely, capturing some prisoners and much property, among which were the very guns that were lost on the Peninsula from the battery he then commanded.

Returning, he reported the enemy as in full flight, and on the 20th Porter prepared to give immediate chase. A part of one of his divisions had crossed the ford and gained the bluffs on the right bank. Our own brigade was on the high lands of the other bank, when, looking across we saw the woods swarm out with rebel infantry rushing upon our little force. A sharp cannonade checked them and covered the return of nearly all our regiments, but the 108th Pennsylvania was cut off from the road to the river crossing, and forced to retire up a rising ground, terminating at the river in a high bluff, from which the only escape was to scramble down the steep cliff and thus to gain the ford.

The men poured like a cataract over the edge and down the declivity, and so long as they stayed at its immediate base they were tolerably safe, but their assailants soon gained the edge of the bluff and lying flat, could pick off any who attempted to cross to the Maryland side, and many were killed or wounded and drowned before our eyes.

Our brigade was formed near to the ford; sharp-shooters were placed along the river bank, and the artillery rattled solid shot upon the summit of the bluff. After a time the Pennsylvanians began to run the gauntlet of the ford, but it was several hours before all of them had left the other shore.

In this time many gallant acts were performed, but none more daring than that of the Adjutant of the 108th, who, after reaching the Maryland shore, walked back upon the plate of the dam just above the ford, and standing there midway across the river, exposed from head to heels, shouted the directions to his men as to the manner of their escape from their awkward fix.

When this fight at the ford was over it was near nightfall, and the army encamped along the river side, the pickets of each army occupying its own bank, and for weeks it was all quiet on the Potomac.

VII.

AFTER ANTIETAM.

THE life of a soldier in war-time is made up of alternating seasons of severe toil and of almost absolute idleness. For a few weeks he will be marched to the utmost limit of endurance—will be set to felling forests—building bridges or roads—constructing defences—and then may follow other weeks when his heaviest occupations are made up of drills, parades, and drawing or eating rations.

Such a time of repose was that which we passed on the banks of the Potomac, near Sharpsburg, guarding the line of the Potomac which for lack of heavy autumnal rains was fordable almost anywhere. Generals, quartermasters and commissaries may have been busy, but it was an idle time for the bulk of the army. Stretching for some fifteen miles along the course of the river, the various corps were encamped in due form, the entire regularity of which could be seen from any neighboring eminence. From some such points one could take into view a landscape brilliant with the colors of autumn made yet brighter by the gleam of the orderly array of white tents, and could see the bounds of each regiment, brigade, or division, as if marked upon a map. At night, before tattoo, the lines of lighted tents would show from a distance, like an army of glow-worms.

To supply the wants of the army of men, another army of wagon trains was kept in constant occupation, and the road was soon covered with fine dust, which rose in clouds when it was stirred by the movements of the trains, or by the horses of mounted officers or men; and as these roads extended everywhere among the camps, we lived all day long in an atmosphere of dirt, which when moved by fresh winds, drove and drifted about to our exceeding discomfort. As the weather grew cooler this was increased by the smoke of the camp-fires, until everybody was habitually clothed in dust, and red about the eyes.

Along the picket lines the men of both armies, having agreed not to fire without previous notice, lolled in the sunshine, chaffed each other over the water, and occasionally traded newspapers even, or union coffee for confederate tobacco.

Once in a while there was a foraging expedition or a reconnoissance across the river. In one of these we captured quite a number of prisoners at Shepardstown, chiefly officers and men absent on leave and visiting their friends in that vicinity. One reconnoissance to Leetown occupied two days, and was followed back right sharply by a strong force of the enemy. We remember particularly the fact that on the advance we found where a long-range shell had exploded among a card party of the enemy's men, one or two of whom lay dead with the cards still in their hands.

This uneventful life, aided no doubt by prevalent but not serious bilious disorders, developed in our Regiment a general tendency to homesickness and "hypo." To counteract it several attempts were made to initiate games and athletic exercises among the men, and the officers were requested to set an example to the men by organizing amusements among themselves—but it amounted to nothing, it seemed impossible to induce the men to amuse themselves.

We kept no very careful note of time. One day was pretty much like every other. Sundays were noticeable only for the absence of drills and a little more stupidity. To go home was the height of any-body's ambition.

Private Callahan, of K Company, sought to be discharged for disability—the disability was beyond question, for he was born with it, and he was told by the Surgeon that he ought not to have accepted the bounty for enlistment; that he "ought to be hung" for doing it, to which somewhat severe criticism the soldier retorted that he "would die first." It may not be necessary to state that Callahan was Irish. At Fredericksburg he lost a finger and obtained his coveted discharge.

We were so long here that, as the season advanced, we began to construct defences against the weather, and the acting adjutant even dreamed of a log hut, with a real door and real hinges. The only

artificer at his command was his negro servant, a
man who could admire but could not comprehend
long dictionary words. The Adjutant, directing the
negro as to the construction of the door frame, told
him certain parts were to be perpendicular, others
horizontal, and others parallel; but the black man's
face showed no evidence of comprehension, until
after a dozen different forms of the same instruction
had been resorted to and the master's patience was
exhausted, the idea penetrated the darkened mind of
the servant, who turned upon the officer with the
pertinent remark, "Why, massa, what you wants is
ter have it *true*, ain't it?"

New orders of architecture were rapidly developed, and the manufacture of furniture became an
extensive occupation. It was quite wonderful what
results could be obtained in both of these industries
by the use of barrels and hard-bread boxes. Of the
barrels we made chimneys and chairs; and of the
boxes, tables, washstands, cupboards, and the walls
and clapboards of our dwellings.

We were really getting to be very comfortable in
the latter days of October, 1862, when the orders
began to intimate that we would not live always in
that neighborhood. First, our Company C was de-
tatched for a guard to the reserve artillery, where
it served for ten months. Then, on the 30th, the
whole army drew out like a great serpent, and
moved away down the Potomac to Harper's Ferry,
crossing the river there, then up on the Virginia side,
and along the foot hills of the Blue Ridge.

It was lively times again, and the march was rapid—often forced; but the weather was cool and bracing, and the men were glad of the change. From the 2d to the 15th of November we were on the eastern slopes of the Ridge, and Lee's army in its western valley, racing each for the advantage over the other.

At each gap there was a lively fight for the control of the pass, but we were always ahead, and possession is as many points in war as it is in law. Holding these passes, our movements could be, to a considerable extent, masked from the observation of the enemy, while his were known to our General, whose object was to keep the army of the enemy strung out to the greatest possible length, and at a favorable moment to pounce upon its centre, divide and conquer it.

With the sound of guns almost always in our ears, we raced away through Snickersville, Middlebury, White Plains, and New Baltimore to Warrenton, with little to eat and plenty of exercise. Near White Plains, on the 8th, we marched all day in a snow-storm, and at night, splashed and chilled, bivouacked in a sprout field, making ourselves as comfortable as might be on three or four inches of snow.

Throughout this march the orders were very stringent against straggling and marauding. No allowance was made for transportation of regimental rations except the haversacks of the soldiers, and on the march in cold weather it is a poor (or good)

soldier that does not eat three days' rations in two.
Our changes of base left us often very short of sup-
lies, and it was not in the most amiable mood that
we came to our nightly camp.

Acting-quartermaster Dana, hungering for flesh-
pots, was tempted by the sight of a fat turkey on a
barn-yard fence. The road was a by-way, and not
a soul in sight. Before he could recall the tenor of
the orders, he had covered the bird with his revolver,
but at that moment General Butterfield, with his staff
and escort, following the abrupt turn of the road,
came upon the quartermaster in the very act, and
scared the bird, which flopped heavily down from
the fence and disappeared. To the General's angry
demand for an explanation, Dana quietly replied
that he was about to shoot that " buzzard."

" Buzzard !" roared the General, " that was a turkey, sir." " Was it, indeed ?" replied the innocent
officer ; " how fortunate, General, that you came as
you did, for in two minutes more I should have shot
him for a buzzard." Dana thought that, amid the
laughter which succeeded, he heard the General
describe him as an idiot, but he was not sufficiently
certain about it to warrant charges against the General for unofficer-like language.

The hurried march from Sharpsburg to Warrenton was fruitful in cases of marauding for court-
martial trials, but these courts very generally refused
to convict, on the ground that the men had been so
ill-supplied from our commissariat, that some irregu-
larity was excusable.

One of our sergeants, a butcher by trade, strolling about the woods, came upon a party of men who had captured and killed, and were about cutting up, a rebel pig. Shocked at the unskilful way in which they were operating, our sergeant volunteered his advice and services, which were gratefully accepted. In the midst of the operation the party was surprised by one of the · brigade staff, and the non-commissioned officer, being tried by court-martial, was by its sentence reduced to the ranks and deprived of six months' pay. The story ends sadly, for his mortification from loss of rank, and possibly his anxiety from fear that his family might suffer from the loss of pay, caused him to droop and die.

One of our men, returning from a private foraging expedition laden with a heavy leg of beef, was captured by the provost guard, and, by order of General Griffin, was kept all day "walking post," with the beef on his shoulder, in front of the headquarters' tents. As the General passed his beat he would occasionally entertain him with some question as to the price of beef, or the state of the provision trade, and at retreat the man, *minus his beef*, was sent down to his regiment " for proper punishment," which his commanding officer concluded that he had already received.

Yet another soldier was sent to our headquarters by the Colonel of the Ninth Massachusetts, with the statement that he had been arrested for marauding. Upon cross-examination of the culprit it

I

appeared that he had been captured with a quarter
of veal in his possession by the provost guard of
the Ninth Regiment. A regimental provost guard
was a novelty in the army, but when, on further
questioning, it 'appeared that the offending soldier
had been compelled to leave the veal at Colonel
Guiney's quarters, the advantage of such an organization in hungry times to the headquarters' mess was
apparent, and our Colonel at once ordered a provost
guard to be detailed from the Thirty-second, with
orders to capture marauders and turn over their ill-
gotten plunder to his cook. Unhappily, within the
next twenty-four hours, some high General, whose
larder was growing lean, forbade regimental provost guards in general orders.

It was during our stay at Warrenton that General
Griffin requested the attendance of Colonel Parker
and told him, not as an official communication, but
for his personal information, that three officers of
the Thirty-second had, during the previous night,
taken and killed a sheep, the property of a farmer
near by. Of course the Colonel expressed his regret at the occurrence, but he represented to
the General that, inasmuch as the officers of our
regiment were not generally men of abundant
means, and inasmuch as they had received no pay
from their Government for several months, and inasmuch as it was forbidden them to obtain food by
taking it either from the rations of their men or the
property of the enemy, he (the Colonel) would be
glad to know how officers were to live? The

General, utterly astonished at the state of affairs thus
disclosed, asked in return for some suggestion to
relieve the difficulty.   The suggestion made that
officers should be allowed to buy from the commissaries on credit, was, at the request of General
Griffin, embodied in a formal written communication
to him, and by an order the next day from the
headquarters of the army, it became a standing
regulation until the end of the war.

On the 10th of November the Army of the Potomac was massed near Warrenton as if a general
action was at hand, when everybody was surprised
by the announcement of the removal of General
McClellan from its command.   It was a sad day
among the camps.   The troops turned out at nine
o'clock, bordering the road, each regiment in
doubled column, and General McClellan, followed
by all the generals with their staffs, a cortege of a
hundred or more mounted officers, rode through the
lines, saluted and cheered continually.

It happened that the 32d was the first regiment
to be reviewed.   Being a regiment of soldiers, it
was accustomed to salute its officers in a soldierly
way, and on this occasion was, probably, the only
battalion in the army that did not cheer "Little
Mac," but stood steadily, with arms presented, colors
drooping, and drums beating.   From the surprised
expression on the General's face, it was evident that
for a moment he feared that he had overrated the
good-will of his troops.   The incident, though really
creditable to the Regiment, was considered as a

slight to the General, and for a time was the cause of considerable feeling against the 32d. Even the politics of its commander could not prevent its being stigmatized as an "Abolition concern."

At noon the officers of the Fifth corps were received by General McClellan, who shook hands with all, and at the close of the reception said, his voice broken with emotion: "Gentlemen, I hardly know how to bid you good-bye. We have been so long together that it is very hard. Whatever fate may await me I shall never be able to think of my-self except as belonging to the Army of the Potomac. For what you have done history will do you justice—this generation never will. I must say it. 'Good-bye.'" And so the army parted from the first, the most trusted, and the ablest of its commanders.

VIII.

TO FREDERICKSBURG.

GENERAL BURNSIDE assumed the command and we remained quiet for a week, then moved slowly away toward Falmouth and Fredricksburg, where we arrived on the 22d of November, and encamped near Potomac Creek, at a place afterwards known as "Stoneman's Switch." This camp was destined to be our home for nearly six months, but the popular prejudice against winter quarters was so great that we were never allowed to feel that it was more than a temporary camp.

On several occasions we had suffered for want of supplies, generally not more than for a day or two, and when on the march; but for ten days after our arrival near Fredericksburg, the whole army was on short allowance. Our base was supposed to be at Acquia Creek, but the railroad was not reconstructed and what supplies we got were wagoned up some miles from Belle Plain, over or through roads which were alternately boggy with mud, or rough with the frozen inequalities of what had been a miry way.

Little by little the scarcity became more severe; for a week there had been no meat-ration, nothing

117 .

was issued except hard-bread, and on the morning
of Thanksgiving Day, there was absolutely no food
for the Regiment.   The evening previous, one box
of hard-bread, the last remainder of the supply of
the headquarters' mess was issued to the Regiment,
giving one half of a cracker to each man, and this
was gratefully received.

That Thanskgiving Day dawned upon a famished
and almost mutinous army.   Rude signs were set
up in the camp, such as "Camp Starvation,"
"Death's Headquarters," "Misery."   Every General
as he appeared, was hailed with cries for "hard-
bread, hard-bread!" and matters looked threatening.
In the 32d there was no disturbance, but the men sat
about with moody looks and faces wan with hunger.
Officers had been despatched in every direction in
search of food but, it was high noon before even hard-
biscuit could be obtained.   Then twenty boxes were
procured by borrowing from the regular division,
and they were brought to our camp from a distance of
two miles, on the shoulders of our men.

That morning the breakfast table of the field and
staff mess, exhibited a small plate of fried hard-
bread and another of beefsteak, obtained by incred-
ible exertions of the Adjutant the day before, in
order to do honor to the festival.   One must be very
hungry to know how sumptuous the repast appeared,
but none of us could eat while the soldiers were
starving, and the breakfast was sent to the hospital
tent.

One man refused to do duty, declaring that the
government had agreed to pay, clothe, and feed him,

and having left him penniless, ragged, and starving
with cold and hunger, he could not be expected to
keep his part of the contract. With this one exception the bearing of our men was superb, and was
in remarkable contrast with that of the army in
general.

At the company roll call at "retreat," the soldier just
referred to, who had been in confinement all day,
was marched through the camp under guard, and
made to face each company in succession, while a
regimental order was read acknowledging and
thanking the men for their good behavior under trying circumstances, and closing with the declaration
that "if on this day of Thanksgiving we have failed
to enjoy the abundance which has usually marked
the festival, we have at least one reason for thankfulness and that is, that when all of us were hungry
there was only one man who desired to shirk his
duty, leaving it to be done by his equally-hungry
comrades, and that the name of that man was— —.

Notwithstanding the repeated declarations that
there would be no winter quarters short of Richmond, the army proceeded to make itself as comfortable as possible. The woods melted rapidly to
supply the great camp-fires, now needed for warmth
as well as cooking; and the soldiers, organizing
themselves into messes, built shelters more satisfactory than the canvas which was provided for that
purpose.

Great variety of ingenuity was exhibited in the
construction of these quarters. A few were content

with an excavation in the ground, over which would be pitched a roofing of tent cloth; but some of the quarters rose almost to the dignity of cottages, having walls of logs, the interstices closed by a plastering of clay, and roofs of rough-hewn slabs, or thatched with branches of pine. Windows were covered by canvas, and chimneys were built up cob fashion and plastered inside, and comfortable fires blazed upon the hearths.

About the headquarters of the generals were enclosing fences of sapling pines set into the ground upright, and held firmly in that position. Within the enclosures were grouped the tents of the general, his staff, and their servants, some of them having outer walls of boards enclosing the sides of their wall tents.

The weather was of a variety indescribable, except as Virginia weather — alternating periods of cold so severe as to freeze men on picket duty, and so warm as to make overcoats an insupportable burden. The rains made the earth everywhere miry, then it would freeze the uneven mud to the hardness of stone, then a thaw made everything mud and all travel impossible, and presently dry winds would convert all into dust and blow about in clouds.

One of the wonders of these times was the army cough; what with the smoke of the camp fires, the dust of the country, and the effect of the variable weather upon people living out of doors, there was a general tendency to bronchial irritations, which would break out into coughing when the men first awoke, and it is almost a literal fact, that when one hundred thousand men began to stir at reveille, the sound of their coughing would drown that of the beating drums.

Here for three weeks in preparation for another movement "on to Richmond," we drilled, were inspected and reviewed — relieving these severer duties by chopping, hauling, and burning wood.

Those of us who had the opportunity, occasionally went over toward the river, where from the high lands we could watch the Confederate lines, and look on to see them getting the opposite heights good and strong in readiness for our attack.

On the 10th of December, the orders began to read as if they really meant fight, and the great point of interest in our discussions was as to the direction of the next movement — whether we were to flank Lee by way of the fords of the Rappahannock as was generally believed, or whether, as some said, we were to embark for Harrison's Landing or City Point, and flank Richmond itself.

No voice was heard to intimate that any such consummate folly could be intended as to attack squarely in face those defenses which we had apparently been quite willing to allow our enemy to construct, and for weeks most deliberately to strengthen. But such was indeed the forlorn hope imposed upon the Army of the Potomac.

December 11th, 1862.—Reveille sounded at 3 A. M. The morning was cool and frosty, the ground

frozen, the air perfectly still—so still and of such
barometrical condition that the smoke of the camp-
fires did not rise to any considerable height, and was
not wafted away, but murked the whole country
with its haze, through which objects when visible
looked distorted and ghostly, and the bugles sounding the assembly had a strange and impressive tone.

The first break of day found the brigade formed
for the march. The troops wore their overcoats,
and outside of them were strapped knapsacks, haversacks, cartridge-boxes, and cap-pouches, all filled
to their utmost capacity; and in rolls worn sash-like
over one shoulder and under the other, were their
blankets and the canvas of their *tentes d'arbri*.

The dull boom of two guns from the westward
was evidently a signal, and the bugle sounded
" forward." That day it was the turn of our Regiment to lead the Brigade, and of our Brigade to lead
the Corps, and we were at once *en route* in the
direction of Fredericksburg, which was three miles
away. Soon after the march began the sun rose,
showing at first only its huge, dull-red disk, but
soon rising above the haze, throwing its bright
beams athwart the landscape, making it and us
cheery with their warmth and shine. With the sunrise came a gentle movement of the air, pushing
away the smoke from the uplands, but leaving the
river valley thick with fog. Midway between our
camp and the river we crossed the summit of a
round-topped hill, from which, by reason of the
sweep of the river, we could see for a distance the

rolling lands of Stafford Heights, which on its left bank form the immediate valley of the Rappahannock, and over all these hills, now glowing in the sunlight, were moving in columns of fours, converging, apparently, toward a common centre, the various corps and divisions of the Army of the Potomac, more than a hundred thousand men.

Across the river could be seen, but not as yet distinctly, the fortified line of hills occupied by Lee's Army of Virginia. Between us and them, the river and the river bottoms on the farther side, with all of the town of Fredericksburg except the church spires and the cupola of its Court House, were shrouded in vapor.

General Burnside had established headquarters in the Phillips house, a fine brick mansion overlooking the valley and the town, and our grand division was massed near by in a large field of almost level land, entirely bare of tree or shade, and here we passed the whole day under a warm December sun, which softened the ground into mud, glared in our eyes, and baked our unprotected heads.

Before we reached this spot the dogs of war were in full cry. Down by the river side there were frequent sputterings of musketry, and the hills on either side of the river were roaring with the sound of the great guns from their earth-work batteries.

About the Phillips house, on its piazza and in its rooms, there were gatherings of general and field officers, discussing with more or less warmth the situation and the probabilities. Occasionally a mounted officer or orderly would come dashing up from the river side, looking hot and anxious, and after delivering or receiving reports or orders, would hasten down again to his station; but, on the whole, things were very deliberately done.

When the fog lifted, below us, and directly on our bank of the stream, could be seen the hospitable-looking Lacy house with its low wings, under the lee of which, sheltered from the fire of the enemy, were groups of officers, their horses picketed in the dooryard. On the opposite side of the river, its houses coming close down to high-water mark, lay the compactly built town of Fredericksburg; beyond it a space of level land, narrowing at the upper end of the town to nothing, but opening below into a wide plain, which, so far as we could see, was everywhere bounded to the west by a rise of land more or less abrupt, forming the lip of the valley there. This rising land terminated just above the town, in a bluff at the river bank.

The right and centre grand divisions of Burnside's army occupied the heights on the eastern side of the river. Lee's forces were entrenched in those on the western side. Between them, the River Rappahannock and the city of Fredericksburg.

The left grand division, under Franklin, one or two miles down the river, before 10 o'clock had laid pontoon bridges and secured a foot-hold on the opposite shore. Between him and the enemy was a nearly open plain, the extent of which, from the river to the rising ground, was more than a mile.

On our left everything had gone smoothly and well; all opposition to the crossing had been easily overcome, but in the immediate front of the town it was quite another story.

At early dawn the engineers were ready and began to lay the pontoon bridges opposite the town. A dozen or more of the boats had been moored into position, and men were actively at work laying plank across, when Barksdale's Mississippians opened fire and drove the Union men to cover. Calling up a brigade of Hancock's men to cover the work, repeated attempts were made to bridge the river, but the Confederates occupying the houses on their bank could fire from windows without being seen themselves, and the endeavors of the engineers, although gallantly made, were unsuccessful.

Then followed a long consultation at headquarters, which resulted in an order to concentrate the fire of our artillery on Fredericksburg, and for an hour or more a hundred and fifty guns played on the town. Fires broke out in several places and raged without restraint. During and after the cannonade our troops essayed again and again to moor the boats and lay the bridge, but the fire of the enemy, although reduced, was yet too fierce, and at last, about four, P. M., two or three of the boats of the pontoon train were loaded with volunteers and pushed across the river at a bend above the buildings, the rebels were flanked and driven from their shelter, and the bridge was speedily constructed.

To us, three-quarters of a mile away, the delay finally became irksome and the Colonel and Major, moved by curiosity, rode down to the river. The Rappahannock here lies deep between its banks and they rode to the edge of the bluff, peering over, up and down the stream, to see what might be seen. The firing for the time had ceased, and all seemed quiet except the crackling flames of the burning buildings. The gunners of the two-gun battery close by were chatting, leaning lazily against the gun-carriages. Below, the river, waiting the turn of the tide to flood, was still and smooth. Opposite, the warehouses, thrusting their unhandsome walls down to the line of tidal mud, seemed utterly deserted; two or three of them were yet burning, a few were badly battered, but on the whole the storm of shot and shell had done wonderfully little harm.

A rifle ball, passing between the two officers, singing as it went, reminded them that everything was not as peaceful as it seemed, and they turned away just as the battery joined the renewed bombardment to cover the forlorn hope in their boat crossing.

That night we bivouacked in a neighboring wood, where we remained also the next day and night, while Franklin on one side of us, and Sumner on the other, were crossing and deploying their commands below and in the town, covered for the greater part of the day by a dense fog which allowed neither the enemy nor us to see much of the movements.

General Burnside would seem to have had an idea that he could push his army across the river, attack Lee's army and win the heights, before Jackson, from his position eighteen miles below, could come to aid his chief. This possibly might have been done by flanking, if he had been content to cross the Rappahannock where Franklin, at 9 o'clock on the 11th, had succeeded in establishing his bridges; but before the upper pontoon bridges could be laid, the rebel right wing, under Jackson, had effected its junction with the lines of Longstreet, and Lee's army was again united.

December 13th, 1862,—the day of the battle of Fredericksburg,—opened clear and bright, except that over the lowlands bordering the river was stretched a veil of vapor which laid there until 9 o'clock. The grand divisions of Sumner and Franklin were over the river and ready for battle—Sumner in the streets of Fredericksburg, which ran parallel to the river, and Franklin in the open plain below the town. Our (Hooker's) grand division yet occupied the heights on the eastern side of the Rappahannock, from which—except for the fog—could be seen the slightly undulating plain, which was to be Franklin's field of battle, but from which the greater part of Sumner's field was hidden by the town itself.

The letter A may be used to demonstrate the topography of the battle. The left limb of that letter may represent the line of higher land occupied by the Confederates, the right limb the line of the

Rappahannock river, and the cross-bar the course
of a sunken creek which separated the lines of
Sumner's troops from those of Franklin, but which
offered no advantage to our troops, and no impedi-
ment to the fire of either of the combatants. Below
the cross-bar of the A, the space between the limbs
may have averaged two-thirds of a mile in width,
over which Franklin's men must advance to the
attack, almost constantly exposed to the fire from
the batteries of the rebels, and for at least half the
way to that from the rifles of their infantry. Within
the triangle—the upper portion of the A—was included the city of Fredericksburg and Sumner's
aceldama, and here the lines of the enemy were
strengthened by earthworks on the summit of the
heights, (not fifty feet above the level of the plain),
and by stone walls and rifle pits along their base.
Here the space between the foremost rebel line, and
the nearest blocks of houses in the town was nowhere
two thousand feet, and within this narrow space,
under the fire of a mile of batteries, and at least
ten thousand rifles, the Union lines must be formed
for the attack.

What we saw of Franklin's battle was what happened before noon, and after 9 o'clock,—at which
latter hour the fog disappeared, revealing to us and
to the enemy the advancing line of Meade's division,
to us a moving strip of blue on the dun-colored plain.
We saw it halt, covered no doubt by some undula-
tion of the land, while a battery on the left was
silenced by the Union guns—then the line moved

on, fringed sometimes with the smoke of its own volleys, at other times with the silver-like sheen of the rifle barrels. We saw the smoke of the rebel rifles burst from the woods that covered the first rise of ground—saw Meade's line disappear in the woods, followed by at least one other line,—then our bugles called "attention! forward!" and we saw no more of Franklin's fight.

Early in the morning two of Hooker's divisions had been sent to strengthen Franklin, and now two others, Humphrey's and Griffins' (ours) were ordered to the support of Sumner. A new boat-bridge had been laid, crossing the river at the lower part of the town, just below the naked piers of what had been and is now the railroad bridge, and just above the outlet of a small stream. The two divisions were massed on the hill-side near this bridge—an attractive mark for the rebel cannoneers, who however, having food for powder close at hand, spared to us only occasionally a shell. The crossing must have occupied an hour. Down the steep hill-side and the steeper bank; over the river and toiling up the western side; with many waits and hitches—the serpent-like column moved tediously along. Once up the bank, and the rifle balls whistled about us and our casualties began; but we wound our way, bearing a little to the left, through the lower portion of the town, where the buildings were detached and open lots were frequent, availing ourselves of such cover as could be used, until in a vacant hollow each regiment as it came up was halted to

J

leave its knapsacks and blankets. These were
bestowed in heaps, and the men and boys of the
drum-corps were left to guard them. Here too,
by order of the Colonel, the field and staff officers
dismounted, leaving their horses in charge of servants. Then in fighting trim we moved forward past
the last buildings, out upon the field of battle. Here
was still between us and the enemy a swell of land,
six or eight feet in its greatest height, affording some
slight protection, and we trailed our arms to conceal
our presence from the enemy.

The confusing roar of the battle was all about us.
Our own batteries of heavy guns from Stafford
Heights were firing over us—a few of our field
pieces were in action near by. The rebel guns all
along their line were actively at work—their shells
exploded all around us, or crashed into the walls of
neighboring buildings, dropping fragments at every
crash; whatever room there might have been in the
atmosphere for other noise, was filled by the rattle
of musketry and the shouts of men.

No words can fully convey to a reader's mind the
confusion which exists when one is near enough to
see and know the details of battle. One reads with
interest in the reports of the generals, the letters of
newspaper correspondents, or in the later histories
constructed from those sources, a clear story of
what was done; of formations and movements as if
they were those of the parade; of attack and
repulse—so graphically and carefully described as
to leave clear pictures in one's mind. But it may be

doubted whether one who was actively engaged, and in the thick of the fight, can correctly describe that which occurred about him, or tell with any degree of accuracy the order of events or the time consumed.

The reports of the battle of Fredericksburg describe occurrences that never happened, movements that were never made, incidents that were impossible. "History" tells how six brigades formed for attack on our right, in column of brigades, with intervals of two hundred paces—where no such formation was possible, and no such space existed. And at least one general (Meagher), in his reports must have depended much upon imagination for the facts so glowingly described.

To the memory now comes a strange jumble of such situations and occurrences as do not appear in the battles of history or of fiction. Of our Regiment separated from the rest of the brigade, getting into such positions that it was equally a matter of wonder that we should ever have gone there, or having gone should ever have escaped alive—of rejoining the division, where, one behind the other and close together in the railroad cut, were three brigades waiting the order for attack.

We recall the terrific accession to the roar of battle with which the enemy welcomed each brigade before us as it left the cover of the cut, and with which at last it welcomed us. We remember the rush across that open field where, in ten minutes, every tenth man was killed or wounded, and where

Marshall Davis, carrying the flag, was, for those minutes, the fastest traveller in the line; and the Colonel wondering, calls to mind the fact that he saw men in the midst of the severest fire, stoop to pick the leaves of cabbages as they swept along.

We remember how, coming up with the 62d Pennsylvania of our brigade, their ammunition exhausted and the men lying flat on the earth for protection, our men, proudly disdaining cover, stood every man erect and with steady file-firing kept the rebels down behind the cover of their stone wall, and held the position until nightfall. And it was a pleasant consequence to this that the men of the gallant 62d, who had before been almost foes, were ever after our fast friends.

Night closed upon a bloody field. A battle of which there seems to have been no plan, had been fought with no strategic result. The line of the rebel infantry at the stone wall in our front was precisely where it was in the morning. We were not forty yards from it, shielded only by a slight roll of the land from the fire of their riflemen, and so close to their batteries on the higher land that the guns could not be depressed to bear on us. At night our pickets were within ten yards of the enemy.

Here we passed the night, sleeping, if at all, in the mud, and literally on our arms. Happily for all, and especially for the wounded, the night was warm. In the night our supply of ammunition was replenished, and toward morning orders were received not to recommence the action.

The next day, a bright and beautiful Sunday, there was comparative quiet along the lines, but to prevent the enemy from trees or houses or from vantage spots of higher land bringing to bear upon our line the rifles of their sharp-shooters, required constant watchfulness and an almost constant dropping fire from our side.

Several attempts were made to communicate with us from the town, but every such endeavor drew a withering fire from the enemy. None of us could stand erect without drawing a hail of rifle balls. A single field-piece from the corner of two streets in the city exchanged a few shots over our heads with one of the batteries on the heights, but soon got the worst of it and retired.

Sergeant Spalding, in a printed description of this day, says: "It was impossible for the men in our brigade to obtain water without crossing the plain below us, which was a hazardous thing to attempt to do, as he who ventured was sure to draw the enemy's fire; nevertheless, it was not an uncommon thing to see a comrade take a lot of canteens and run the gauntlet. Seldom were they hit, but in a few instances we saw them fall, pierced by the rebel bullet.

"I remember seeing a soldier approaching us from the city, with knapsack on his back and gun on his shoulder. I watched him with special interest as he advanced, knowing that he was liable to be fired upon as soon as he came within range of the enemy's rifles. He came deliberately along, climbed over the fence, and was coming directly towards where we lay, when crack went a rifle and down went the man—killed, as we supposed, for he lay perfectly still. But not so, he was only playing possum. Doubtless he thought that by feigning to be dead for a few moments he would escape the notice of the enemy. So it proved, for unexpectedly to us, and I doubt not to the man who shot him (as he supposed), he sprang to his feet and reached the cover of the hill before another shot was fired."

The day wore away and the night came again, and we, relieved by other troops, returned to refresh ourselves by sleeping on the wet sidewalks of one of the city streets.

The next day three lines of infantry were massed in this street, which ran parallel to the river, but the day passed without any renewal of the battle. It was not pleasant, looking down the long street so full of soldiers, to think what might happen if the rebel guns, less than a thousand yards away, should open on the town—but it was none of our business. As it came on to storm at nightfall we took military possession of a block of stores, and the men, for the first time for many months, slept under the cover of a roof. It was a fearfully windy night, and whether it was the wind, or anxiety about the situation, the Colonel could not sleep. His horses were kept in the street conveniently at hand, and once or twice he rode out to the front and heard Captain Martin objurgating the General for his orders to entrench his battery with one pick and one shovel.

About 3 A. M. came an orderly seeking the commander of the brigade, whom nobody had seen for the past two days. The Colonel was inclined to be gruff until he learned that the orders were to move the brigade back over the river; then, indeed, he was sprightly. Declaring himself the ranking officer of the brigade, he receipted for the order and, sending his orders to the other regiments, began to retire the brigade to the easterly bank, and thence ordered the regiments to their old camps at Stoneman's Switch, where the real brigadier found them soon after dawn.

At 8 A. M. Burnside had withdrawn his entire army and taken up his bridges. The storm was over, but again the fog filled the low lands. As it cleared away, some of us, from the piazza of the Phillips House, saw the rebel skirmishers cautiously creeping toward the town, and it was not long before the shouts from their lines told that the evacuation was discovered. In the battle of Fredericksburg the 32d lost thirty-five killed and wounded. Among the killed was Captain Charles A. Dearborn, Jr.

IX.

BETWEEN CAMPAIGNS.

WITH the close of the year 1862, Colonel Parker
resigned the command, Lieutenant-Colonel
Prescott was promoted to the Colonelcy; Major
Stephenson was made Lieutenant Colonel, and
Captain Edmunds, Major.

A vacancy occurred also in the medical staff, by
the resignation of Assistant Surgeon Bigelow, and
an elderly, but very respectable M. D. was gazetted
in his place. It happened that the new doctor
reported for duty on the eve of a movement of the
corps. He had no horse; said he had left his
trunk at "the depot," meaning by the roadside, at
Stoneman's Switch, and when told that he must
march with the Regiment next day he undertook to
hire a buggy. The young gentlemen of the Regiment kept him floundering about for a good part of
the night in search of an imaginary livery stable,
and even sent him up to division headquarters to
borrow the General's barouche. One day's experience was enough for him, and the next morning
he declined to be mustered in and went back—he
and his trunk—to the more congenial white set-
tlements.

After the disastrous attempt upon the heights of Fredericksburg, the Regiment had remained in their old camping-ground near Stoneman's Switch, in the neighborhood of Falmouth. Excepting the reconnoissance to Morrisville and skirmish there, with that terrible march on the return when our brigadier, Schweitzer, led his "greyhounds," as he termed them, at such a terrific pace for twenty-five or thirty miles, nothing occurred to break the monotony of camp life. The night of the 31st December, 1862 — that of the march above alluded to — was extremely cold, and the men, in light marching order, without knapsacks or necessary blankets, compelled to fall out from inability to keep the pace, suffered terribly from exposure, and many lost their lives in consequence.

For two months, or since November 22d, 1862, we had been comfortably encamped (including the episodes of the battle of Fredericksburg, and the march and skirmish of Morrisville above-mentioned) near Stoneman's Switch — two months ! which seemed so near an age, a cycle, or an eternity of time in the Army of the Potomac in those days, that we had prepared ourselves as if to remain forever. Our tents were converted into comfortable huts, with wide chimneys and wooden floors; we had tables and camp-chairs and bedsteads and looking-glasses — all rather rudely constructed, perhaps, but to our minds luxurious to a degree unprecedented. When, however, we got marching orders, every man seemed to vie with his neighbor in displaying his contempt for all this effeminacy, and his readiness to quit these "piping times of peace," by destroying all his possessions that savored of luxury, and throwing away whatever could not be carried in knapsack or saddle-pack.

Adjutant Cobb was a sound sleeper. He did not average to sleep so long, perhaps, as many others, but he would owl over his work or his letters night after night, and then, when the conditions were favorable, would do such solid sleeping for one night as would bring him out even. At such times it seemed absolutely impossible to awaken him; no quantity of shaking would make any impression, and it was necessary to let him have it out.

Somewhere about midnight, before January 21st, an orderly came with a written order, found the adjutant sleeping in his tent, and did his best to waken him, but without effect. Finally he thrust the order into Cobb's hand, closed the fingers over it, and went his way. Before daylight the adjutant was wakened by the beating drums, and found the paper in his hand. Rising, he struck a light, read the paper and found that it was an order for the Regiment to march at 3 A. M. It was then half-past two, and an hour and a half is the shortest time in which a command can get breakfast and make needful preparations for the route.

Matters were hurried up pretty lively, and inasmuch as there was the usual delay in starting, the Regiment managed to come to time.

We did not move until four. Meantime the work of destruction went on, even to making bonfires of all comforts and luxuries in wood, around which the men warmed themselves and laughed and sung. Even tent-cloths and cast-off clothing were destroyed. Nothing was to be left that would comfort Johnny Reb. But even before we moved off, some of us began to regret our comfortable home ; for a bitter cold north-east wind blew fiercely, and the air was full of snow and sleet, which gradually grew to rain. We moved at first pretty fast, and then the pace grew slower, slower, slowest, with frequent halts, until after dark, when we drew off the road and bivouacked for the night. The rain continued for some time, and it was exceedingly chilly, and by no means an agreeable opportunity for sleep. The men made fires among the trees, and sat around them nearly all night. As morning rose the wind changed, the rain ceased and when we resumed our march at about eight o'clock the air was soft, bland, and beautiful, like a day in April or May. Heavy, lead-colored clouds, however, hung low over everything, the air was thick with mist, and vaporous masses of steam lay upon the fields and woods. The snow had disappeared, and the frost was coming out of the ground, and lay in pools and puddles, and finally, in lakes and rivers of water, over roads and low-lying fields in every direction. Soon it began raining again, first a drizzle and then a steady pour, and the thermometer rose and rose and rose again, to fifty, seventy, and eighty degrees, every object in the landscape began to exhale steam. Men and horses and mules and wagons, every bush and blade of grass, gave it forth in clouds and masses. There was a glow everywhere as of early dawn, and a dank, earthy smell pervaded the air. The wagons and trains, and everything that went on wheels or by horse-flesh, abandoned the roads and took to the fields. Deeper grew the mud and deeper the water over the mud. Still the moving masses of men pushed on, jumping from hummock to stump, sinking in up to the thighs and being dragged out half drowned, struggling through dense thickets rather than try the road, and everything and everybody draggled and splashed and yellow with mud; there had been something very much like this in the march up the Peninsula under McClellan, in the trenches and corduroys about Yorktown, and we did not expect to give it up. But at last we came to a dead standstill. We were in a narrow wood-road and had passed several teams of a wagon train completely mired, and apparently sinking deeper and deeper, mules singing their peculiar lay with little above the mud but their ears, when we were halted where the road made a sudden turn and descent, and for the present at least, all further progress was impossible. Our entire day's march was only three miles.

The narrow road appeared to be blocked, wagons were upset apparently one upon another, while men and horses were floundering about in most dire confusion. In a very short time we made our way out of this scene of disorder, and to the great relief of all who progressed by horse-flesh, halted to wait a more agreeable season. Then again did we regret the comfortable quarters we had left.

It was dreadful to think of camping where we were, worse to undertake to go back again, or forward or anywhere. The whole country in all directions appeared to be under water. The trees stood up as if in a vast bog or swamp. At the first step off from a root or stump you sank so deep as to make you catch your breath, and you were lucky if, in extracting yourself, you did not leave behind both boots and stockings. Virginia mud is a clay of reddish color and sticky consistence, which does not appear to soak water, or mingle with it, but simply to hold it, becoming softer and softer, and parting with the water wholly by evaporation. It was difficult to stand; to sit or lie down, except in the sticky mud, was impossible. Everything was so drenched with water that it was difficult to make fires. The warm, moist atmosphere imparted a feeling of weariness and lassitude, and in short our condition was disgusting. Wet through, stuck-in-the-mud, we dragged out the night.

The next day, January 23d, was bright, mild, and beautiful, at least as far as sun and air went. A gentle breeze began to dry up the ground, and the whole brigade was set at work to corduroy roads. The method pursued by our own men was peculiar. They were marched across the field and brought into single line before a Virginia fence. Every man then pulled out a rail, shouldered it, and in single file the Regiment marched to the place to be corduroyed, where each dropped his rail as he came up.

The next day we returned to our camp at Stoneman's Switch, which looked on the whole about as comfortable and home-like as the inside of a very mouldy Stilton cheese. In an incredibly short space of time however, everything resumed its accustomed air of neatness and quasi-comfort. The next Sunday-morning inspection showed not a trace of the mud in which the Regiment with the rest of the army had been nearly smothered.

Youthful readers of Lovers' romances are apt to jump at the conclusion that "a soldier's life is always gay," or at least that gaiety is its normal condition. Youthful patriots in our war time yearned for active service, and saw themselves in dreams successfully storming forts, capturing batteries, charging and driving rebel hordes. Always in their dreams there was floating over them the flag of their country, (a bright new one)—always drums were beating and bands were playing ; and, if the dream was dreamed out to the end, the great transformation-scene at the close, displayed the dreamer in elegant uniform, crowned by the genius of victory, while the people of the whole nation joined in shouts of approbation.

As they approached the field of glory the halo faded, and often upon the field itself it was not at all manifest to the eye. A disordered liver turned the gold to green, and the arm which by the dream was to have been waving a flashing sword in the front part of battle, was more frequently wielding a dull axe in the woods, or a spade in the open ground. Many thought that their patriotism had evaporated, but it was only the romantic aureola that was gone.

Among the first volunteers to join our Newton Company was the Reverend William L. Gilman, a minister of the Universalist denomination. To us he was Corporal Gilman of Company K, doing his duty as a non-commissioned officer quietly and well. On the 10th of December, 1862, the Colonel was in the dumps. He had been for two months wrestling with the medical authorities of the corps, and the medical authorities had near about killed him. Upon the eve of a movement and a battle, they refused permission to send our sick to hospital, and ordered our surgeons to follow the movement. More than twenty men were very sick in our hospital tent, and the steward objected to the heavy load which would fall to him if he were left alone in charge.

At this juncture appeared Corporal Gilman with a sad countenance, and told how disappointed he was to find that his services seemed to be of no value, and to ask if some position could not be found in which he might have the satisfaction of feeling that he was of use to somebody. A brief consultation with the Surgeon told the Colonel that the corporal was in no state for marching or fighting, that his despondency was the effect of a disordered liver, and thereupon he was detailed to the military command of the patients in hospital, and before the regiment left he was fully instructed as to the duty required of him. To Corporal Gilman's activity during the five days of our absence, is due a large share of the credit of saving the lives of those entrusted to his care. Shamefully neglected by the division surgeon who promised to visit them, and who even falsely said that he had visited them, these sick men would have died of starvation but for the unwearying devotion of their two non-commissioned officers; and when the regiment returned, Gilman himself was well, and had recovered that cheeriness which was his natural temper, and which never afterward deserted him, even when mangled and dying on the field of Gettysburg.

But after all there was some foundation for those youthful views. There were men who could stand up against their own livers, and there were times of general jollity.

Making a neighborly call at the headquarters of an Irish regiment, our Adjutant found there quite a number of officers, the greater number of them sitting or reclining on the ground, which formed the tent floor, among them Captain Hart, A. A. General of the Irish Brigade.

Of course the canteen was at once produced, and a single glass which was to go the rounds with the canteen. The whiskey was of the "ragged edge" variety, from the commissary stores, and it required a stout throat to drink it half-and-half with water; but when our adjutant, to whom by reason of infirmity of the lungs whiskey was like milk, filled the little glass with clear spirit and tossed it down his throat, there was a murmur of admiring surprise which found expression in Hart's reverent look and in his exclamation, " Oh, sir ! you ought to belong to the Irish Brigade, for it's a beautiful swallow you have !"

But the Irish had no monopoly of light-hearted soldiers. Dana of " ours " was to the battalion what Tupper says a babe is to the household—a well-spring of joy. Full of healthy life and spirits, he bubbled over with jokes and pranks and mirth, and while no story of the 32d could be complete without some stories of him, no one book could suffice to contain them all.

Sent out with a party to corduroy a road, he announced himself at the farm house near by as General Burnside, and demanded quarters, got them, and fared sumptuously.

Detailed as acting quartermaster he kept no accounts, and how he settled with his department no man knoweth to this day. The demand of the ordnance department for property returns, although frequently repeated, were quietly ignored, until the chief wrote to him : " Having no replies to my repeated demands for your accounts, I have this day addressed a communication to the 2d Auditor of the Treasury, requesting him to withhold farther payments to you." To which D. at once replied: " Dear Sir,—Yours of the —th is received. What did the 2d Auditor say ?"

A representative of the Christian Commission in clerical dress and stove-pipe hat was distributing

K

lemons to the bilious soldiers, but refused to give or sell one to Dana, who thereupon proposed to arrest him as a deserter from our army or a spy of the enemy's; and when the gentleman asserted that he was enlisted only in "the army of the Lord"— "Well, you've straggled a good ways from that," was the surly rejoinder.

Sergeant Hyde of K Company was a Yankee given to the invention of labor-saving contrivances, and was not fond of walking two miles under a big log, which was then the ordinary process of obtaining fire-wood. He thought that he might get his fuel with less labor, from the generous pile which always flanked the surgeon's tent. Getting one of his comrades, in the darkness of night, to draw off the attention of the headquarters' negro servants, Hyde secured a boss log and escaped with it to his hut, and there, with the aid of a newly-issued hatchet, proceeded to demolish his log beyond the possibility of recognition.

Unfortunately for Hyde, the sharp hatchet glanced off the log and cut an ugly gash in his leg—a serious wound, which made it necessary to call on the surgeon and break his rest. The doctor was kind and sympathizing beyond his wont, and very curious to learn all about the accident, but to this day the sergeant believes that if that doctor had known all the particulars, the treatment might not have been so gentle.

Whenever the army was idle for a time, officers were apt to be prolific in written communications, recommendations, and endorsements, and these were not always merely dry routine. The officer of the guard who knew more about tactics than any other learning, one day on his report wrote a suggestion that ".sum spaids and piks" be provided for the use of the guard. This passing as usual through the hands of the officer-of-the-day, who knew more about books than tactics, he added over his official signature, "approved all but the spelling."

A. Q. M. Hoyt having in a written communication to the General of the division called attention to the fact that the division quartermaster was using an ambulance and horses for his own private occasions in violation of an order of the War Department, was by endorsement directed to "attend to his own duty," whereupon he sent the same paper to the Adjutant General at Washington, with this additional endorsement, "In compliance with the above order of Gen. ———— the attention of the War Department is called to the case within described." The ambulance had to go.

It was in one of these prolonged waiting seasons that the assistant surgeon with great exertion at all of the headquarters, secured a thirty days leave of absence in order to be present at his own wedding. Nothing now could make his face so long as it was next morning at the mess breakfast, when an orderly brought, and when the adjutant read aloud a general order from headquarters, Army of the Potomac, cancelling all officers' leaves "pending the present operations of this army." A premature chuckle from one of the conspirators exposed the forgery and lightened the doctor's heart.

It was not in every place and presence however, that even a full surgeon could indulge his natural bent for humorous relation, as indeed the chief of our medical staff discovered, when, after convulsing a Court Martial with a vivid description of a pig hunt, where he came in at the death to find the prisoners cutting up the pig, and the Adjutant General of the division "presiding over the meeting," he found his reward in "plans and specifications," upon which he himself was tried for contempt of court, or something to that effect.

St. Patrick's Day was always a day of great jollity, for the religious children of that holy bishop and his cherished isle are quick to break forth into mirth and sport when opportunity is offered. The festival of 1863, however, closed with a strange accident and a sad tragedy.

A course had been provided for horse racing, and after the races laid down in the programme had been run, a variety of scrub matches were made up *extempore*. Unfortunately, it happened that two of these were under way at the same time and in opposite directions, and at the height of their speed, two horses came in collision so directly, and with such a fearful shock as to cause the instant death of both animals, the actual death of one, and the apparent death of both the riders. He who escaped at last, was the dear foe of our Quartermaster

Hoyt, who, over the senseless body pronounced the officer's eulogy, and expressed his deep contrition for all that he had ever said or done to offend the sufferer, but with the reserved proviso that "if he does get well this all goes for nothing."

X.

CHANCELLORSVILLE.

THE commencement of the year 1863 brought the not unwelcome announcement to the Army of the Potomac that General Burnside had been relieved from the command, and General Hooker appointed in his stead. The disastrous failure at Fredericksburg, and the rather absurd attempt which will be known in history as the "mud march," had not increased the confidence of the army in Burnside's ability, and it was with feelings of satisfaction that the soldiers heard the order promulgated which relieved him and appointed his successor. Notwithstanding some grave defects in the character and habits of General Hooker, as a soldier he had enlisted the confidence and won the affections of the men. The plucky qualities which had given to him the name of "Fighting Joe," seemed to be an assurance of that activity and energy that were so necessary to the successful ending of the contest, while his kindly nature, and his genial, social temperament, won the love and good wishes of all who came in contact with him. In appearance, when in command, he represented the dashing, chivalrous soldier, of whom we had read in history and fiction, inspiring confidence and awakening our enthusiasm. As he rode along the line, while reviewing the 5th Corps, mounted upon a snow-white steed, horse and rider seemingly but one, erect in all the pride of command, his hair nearly white, contrasting strongly with his ruddy complexion, he looked the perfect ideal of a dashing, gallant, brave commander. We soon learned that his skill in organization fully equalled his bravery upon the battle-field, and the results were apparent in the improved discipline and *morale* of the troops. To his administration must be given the credit of the introduction of the corps badges, which proved of great value in the succeeding days of the war.

It would be useless, tiresome perhaps, to describe the regular routine performed by the 32d during the days and weeks that succeeded. Suffice it to say, that it consisted principally of picket and guard duty, with details for road building, and the constant drill and discipline so necessary to prepare the soldier for the more severe labors of the march, and the sterner duties of the battle-field. With the warmer weather of the spring came orders which told us that the campaign was soon to begin; baggage must be forwarded to Washington, clothing must be furnished, deficiences in ordnance supplied; these, together with orders for the return of men on leave and detached service, informed the soldier as clearly as if it had been promulgated in positive terms, that active duties were to commence, that a battle was soon to be fought. On the 8th of

April, President Lincoln reviewed the army, and
the sight of a hundred thousand men prepared for
review was indeed impressive.   General Hooker was
excusable, perhaps, in speaking of his command at
this time as "the finest army on the planet."   It certainly was never in better condition.   On the 27th of
April we left our camp—the Regiment under the
command of Lieutenant-Colonel Stephenson—without a thought that we should ever return to it again.
Starting at noon, we marched to Hartwood Church,
about eight miles, reaching it at nightfall; the next
morning, moving towards Kelley's Ford on the Rappahannock, near which we bivouacked for the night;
taking up the line of march at daybreak, we crossed
the Rappahannock on a pontoon bridge, coming to
Ely's Ford on the Rapidan, late in the afternoon of the
29th.   The water at this ford was quite deep, reaching nearly to the armpits, and running rapidly.
Most of the men stripped themselves of their clothing and waded through, holding their muskets,
knapsacks, and clothing above their heads, while
others dashed in without any preparation.   Occasionally a luckless wight would lose his footing in
the swift-running stream, and float down with the
current, to be caught by the cavalry men who were
stationed below for that purpose.   Regiment after
regiment as they arrived, dashed through the waters,
and a more stirring scene can hardly be imagined.
All along the banks of the river were men by hundreds, and thousands—on one side making preparation for fording—on the other replacing their

clothing and repairing damages, while the water was crowded with soldiers who filled the air with shouts, laughter, and song. As the darkness came on, the numerous fires which the soldiers had made for the purpose of drying their clothing, threw a strong light over a picture of life and beauty, such as can only be witnessed in the experience of army life. That night we rested on the south side of the Rapidan. The morning of the 30th of April found us on the march, and in a few hours we struck that region, which, but for the war, would scarcely have been known outside of its own limits — now to be remembered by generations yet to come, as the locality where were fought some of the bloodiest battles known in history — the Wilderness.

Some description of the territory may not come amiss to those who have grown up since the bloody scenes of the war for the Union were enacted there. It comprises a tract of land probably more than twenty miles in circumference; a nearly unbroken expanse of forest and thicket. A large portion is covered with a dense growth of low, scrub oaks, briars, and shrubs, with occasionally a spot where the trees have attained to more lofty proportions. For miles you can travel without a change, seeing only the loathsome snake as it glides across your path, and uncheered by the voices of the birds, for the songsters of the day find no home in its thickets, only the lonely night-bird inhabiting its gloomy depths. Everything about it is wild and desolate. The sun hardly penetrates through its gloom, and the traveller, oppressed with its loneliness and desolation, hurries through that he may reach the more genial spots beyond, and feel the cheering rays of God's sunshine.

Near one border of this region, at the junction of roads that lead from Fredericksburg and United States Ford, is Chancellorsville; not a town, not a village, but simply a tract of cleared land surrounding one brick house, said to have been erected for a private residence, but used at the commencement of the war as a roadside tavern. Through the forest we marched to Chancellorsville, near which we bivouacked for the night.

May 1st, 1863, our Regiment led the division which marched not south-east in the direction of the plank road, but by a road which led east and north-east, in the direction of Bank's Ford. Artillery and picket firing had been heard for some time, but we were in thick woods. Covered by flankers and skirmishers we moved on sometimes very rapidly, until within less than four miles of Fredericksburg. The day was fine and with the exception of some cavalry pickets, we saw no enemy, but there was a sound of heavy firing on our right in the direction of the plank road, and as we advanced it seemed to become more distant and almost exactly in our rear.

By the excitement apparent among General Griffin's staff it was evident that things were not going right, and at last the order was given to face about, and we took the back track at a killing pace. As we neared Chancellorsville again, there was some pretty sharp artillery and infantry skirmishing going on just ahead, and as night drew on we were halted in the road in line of battle facing south, with skirmishers in front.

It seems that the regular division of our corps had been roughly handled and driven back, thus separating us from the army, and we were kept all that night marching and counter-marching about the country. It was a bright moonlight night, but dusky in the woods. There were long waits, but not enough for sleep, and it was long after daylight when we got out of the forest and came upon the 3d division of our corps, and found ourselves welcomed as men who had been lost but were found.

On the morning of May 2d we were posted on the extreme left of the army and ordered to build breastworks. The axe and the spade were soon busily at work, and before night a formidable barrier had been erected against any attack. About sunset there was some slight skirmishing, and the men stood in line awaiting an attack, but none came. All was still as night; not a sound was heard except the low murmuring of voices. Even the dropping fire of the pickets had ceased, when suddenly on our right there burst on the air the sound of a volley of musketry accompanied by the wild rebel yell that was so familiar to the soldier of the Union. From the first it seemed to come towards us like a torrent, constant and resistless. The men stood, musket in hand, peering into the gloom, every nerve strung, ready to meet the attack, but it did not reach us, and ceased suddenly at last. This was the famous flank attack by Stonewall Jackson upon the 11th Corps under General Howard, which was ended thus abruptly by the death of the rebel commander. On the morning of the 3d we relieved and changed positions with the 11th Corps. Our new position was just at the right of Chancellorsville house, by the side of the road; before us a cleared plain probably two hundred yards wide, beyond which was a forest. Again we were ordered to throw up earthworks, and the men were busily at work all day. Our brigade was formed in two lines, the 32d being a part of the front line, where it remained until the army fell back.

About noon on the 4th our brigade received orders to advance across the plain into the woods. That morning a fire had swept through the woods, burning the accumulated leaves, the deposit of years, and in addition to the heat of the day, we suffered from the hot ashes that arose under our footsteps in clouds.

The purpose of this advance was to feel out the enemy and draw his fire, but not to bring on an engagement, the object being to ascertain whether he was still in force on our front. The movement was executed in gallant style. The enemy received us with a hot fire of musketry and artillery, the greater portion of which fortunately went over our heads. We were at once ordered to retire and did so, under a tremendous shower of shot and shell, nearly all of which passed above us.

We remember with pride the precision with which the brigade returned across the field, as coolly as if passing in review, rather than under the fire of the enemy, a movement which elicited the hearty cheers of the division. The most excited individual was a non-commissioned officer who, being lightly hit by a piece of shell as we entered our earthworks, maddened by the stinging pain, turned and shook his fist at the invisible foe, abusing him most lustily, amidst the laughter of his companions. Our advance demonstrated that the enemy was still there, and in a short time they made their appearance in masses issuing from the edge of the wood, but they were received with a fire of artillery that sent them reeling back to their defences, leaving great numbers of dead and wounded on the field.

The morning of the 5th came in with a cold, heavy rain, making our position that day anything but pleasant, but we did not move. As soon as darkness came on, the batteries began to withdraw, then we could hear the tramp of regiment after regiment as they moved away, and we soon learned that the army was retiring across the Rappahannock. Still no orders came for us, and we began to realize that again our division was to cover the retreat, and be the last withdrawn. The ground was soaked with water, we could neither sit nor lie down, but crouching under the little shelter tents, which afforded some protection from the drenching rain, we waited for our turn to come.

It was nearly morning when we started, and sunrise when, after wading through mud and water

often knee deep, we reached United States Ford.
The engineers were in position there ready to take
up the pontoons. Striking swiftly across the country, hungry, tired, and disheartened, we re-occupied
before noon our old quarters at Stoneman's and
the grand movement of General Hooker upon Richmond was ended. The loss of the 32d was only
one killed and four wounded.

XI.

FREDERICKSBURG TO GETTYSBURG.

AFTER the battle of Chancellorsville the whole army retired to its old position about Stafford Court House and Falmouth, on the Rappahannock, opposite the City of Fredericksburg. The 32d Massachusetts was detailed to guard duty along the railroad from Acquia Creek; half of the command under Lieutenant-Colonel Stephenson being posted at or near the redoubts on Potomac Creek, guarding the bridge; the remainder, or right wing, under Colonel Prescott, posted south of Stoneman's Switch.

On Thursday afternoon, May 29th, orders were received to break camp and move to Barnett's Ford. The left wing moved promptly, but the right wing, owing to the temporary absence of Colonel Prescott, did not march until after nightfall. A bright full moon and cool breeze made marching delightful. The way was familiar, the roads fine, and the men, in the best of spirits, laughed and sung as they went. At about midnight this hilarity had subsided, and the little column was jogging sleepily along the way, which wound through a deep wood in the vicinity of Hartwood Church. Suddenly, at a sharp turn of the road, where the moonlight fell bright as

day, came a stern call " Halt ! who goes there?"
and a dozen horsemen, springing from the shadow,
stood barring the way, bringing forward their carbines with a threatening click as they appeared.
The column, however, not halting, pressed forward
into the light, showing the glittering muskets of
the men and something of their number.   The
horsemen seemed to suddenly abandon their purpose, for, without a word of parley, they turned
their horses into the woods and slipped past us
under cover of the darkness. We recognized them,
when too late, as a band of guerillas, and learned
more concerning them at the first picket post we
met.

During our stay at the fords of the Rappahannock,
guerillas harrassed us in various ways, hovering
around us, indeed, until we neared the border of
Maryland. Now a portion of our wagon train
would be run off, and an officer would be spirited
away when on outpost duty or riding from one
camp to another. Again and again the mail was
stopped and rifled, the carrier shot or captured.
Indeed, these things became of so frequent occurrence that stringent orders came from headquarters
forbidding officers or men straying beyond the limits
of their camp guards. Many were the sensational
rumors concerning the guerillas and their Chief
Mosby. One of our cavalry officers used to say that
he never could catch a guerilla, but after a long
chase occasionally found a man wearing spurs, engaged in digging a well.

At Hartwood Church the two wings of the Regiment were again united, and moved on the following day past Barnett's to Kemper's Ford. Mrs. Kemper and her daughter were the only inmates of their mansion, Mr. Kemper being "away," which meant in the rebel army, and of the swarms of servants which no doubt once made the quarters lively, there remained only two or three small girls and an idiot man.

Our stay here was one of the bright spots of army experience. The location was delightful and the duty light. We had a detail on guard at the ford and pickets along the river bank; opposite to us on the other shore, and within talking distance, were the rebel pickets, but no shots were exchanged, and all was peaceful and quiet.

We had extended to the family such protection as common courtesy demanded, and when we were about to leave, a few of the officers called to say good-bye, and found the ladies distressed and in tears on account of our departure, or the dread of what might come afterwards. They told us that ours was the first Massachusetts regiment that had been stationed there; that they had been taught to believe that Massachusetts men were vile and wicked; "but," said one of them, "we have received from no other soldiers such unvarying courtesy and consideration; we have discovered our mistake, and shall know how to defend them from such aspersions in the future." Promising in reply to their urgency that, if taken prisoners and if possible, we would

L

communicate with them, we took our leave, with the impression that it was well to treat even our enemies with kindness.

On the 9th of June occurred the engagement at Brandy Station, said at that time to be the greatest cavalry fight of the war, and the Regiment crossed the river and covered the approaches to the ford while the battle was in progress. They moved out about three miles in the direction of Culpepper Court House, but encountered no enemy, except a few straggling cavalry men, who fled at their approach.

Now the Regiment was kept continually on the *qui vive*, under orders to move at a minute's notice, and be prepared for long and rapid marches.

Suddenly the enemy withdrew all his pickets from the river, and on the 13th of June we moved in the middle of the night, which was very dark, in the direction of Morrisville, and on the following night we reached Catlett's, our division bringing up the rear of the army and guarding the wagon train. The weather had now become very summerlike, and the days were hot and sultry, and the roads heavy with dust. Again we were moving through that detestable Manassas country, that debatable land, now almost a desert; the soil uncultivated, trodden to powder, the fields overgrown with weeds, an arid waste where no water was and no food could be obtained, the breeze stifling one with the pungent odor of penny-royal, which pervaded everything.

June 16th we encamped near Manassas, on the Thoroughfare Gap road, and on the following day

made an ever-memorable march of eighteen or
twenty miles, under a tropical sun, with a stifling
air filled with dust, without a drop of water anywhere, and the men of all ranks and commands
falling down by the roadside and dying of heat-
stroke and exhaustion. The 32d made the best
record of any regiment in the division on this day,
encamping at Gum Spring at night with fuller
ranks than any other. We set out with 230 men
and came in with 107 in the ranks, and even this
poor showing was far ahead of most regiments composing the division. Four soldiers of the division
died from sunstroke on this dreadful march. Firing
was heard all day from the direction of Aldie, and
we were urged forward as rapidly as possible.

On the 19th we moved to Aldie Gap, with the
whole of the 5th Corps, passing many fine places
upon the broad Winchester turnpike. An artillery
skirmish was going on as we neared the Gap at sunset, and we deployed across the broad fields under
the beautiful Blue Ridge mountains in fine style,
bands playing, bugles sounding, etc. At 2 A. M.
on the morning of the 21st the men were awaked,
three days rations issued, and we were soon in
motion up the Gap. As morning broke we defiled
past Aldie, and on the way down the mountain side
were passed by thousands of cavalry, under command of Generals Pleasanton, Gregg, and Kil-
patrick.

During that day and the next we had a glorious
opportunity to witness one of the great cavalry skir-
mishes of the Army of the Potomac, the enemy's

cavalry consisting of Fitz Hugh Lee's brigade led by Rousseau, and Stuart's cavalry led by Stuart himself. We withdrew on the 22d and passed that night near Aldie on the side of the hills, looking down into the valley, and across to Ashby's Gap. Many are the tales since told of what we saw and did during those two days of cavalry and infantry fighting. On the 21st the Regiment led the infantry advance, and on the return was at the rear of the column, and covered the cavalry retreat.

June 26th orders came to move at 3 A. M., and from that time we marched rapidly forward across the state of Maryland, and until we reached the Pennsylvania line.

Early on the afternoon of July 1st, 1863, after a march of about ten miles, the 32d reached Hanover, Pennsylvania, and as we filed into a cleared level piece of grass-land, we congratulated ourselves upon the prospect of a long rest and a refreshing · sleep after the tedious marches and broken slumbers of the previous sixteen days. The men went cheerily to work preparing food, the great difficulty being lack of fuel, for we were in a friendly country, and the usual destruction of fences and trees was forbidden. But we were soon to find ourselves disappointed in our expectations; for, at 8 o'clock, orders came to move, and the men discontentedly packed their knapsacks, giving up all idea of rest so much needed and desired. As we marched toward Gettysburg, we heard in advance the sound of cheering, and soon word came down

the line that General McClellan was again in command of the army.   As the news passed along,
regiment after regiment sent up cheers, and the
soldiers moved with quickened step and joyful
hearts.   Where this report originated we never
knew, yet many went into the battle the next day
thinking they were under the command of the general, who, above all others, had won the love and
confidence of the Army of the Potomac.   Very
soon, orders came for the musicians to give the
time for the march, and we stepped off quickly to
the beat of the drum.   This was one of the very
few occasions on which we used our music while on
the march during the entire service of the Regiment.
Our musicians were used, as a general rule, only in
camp to sound the various calls that marked the
routine of camp duty, and at guard-mountings and
parades, and on this occasion we were allowed but
a few minutes to enjoy the luxury of marching to the
beat of the drum, for it was stopped by orders from
an authority higher than our division general, on
account of the danger of giving information of our
whereabouts to the enemy.

We marched nearly ten miles more that night,
and at midnight bivouacked two miles distant from
the spot that was to be the field of the battle of Gettysburg.   Very early in the morning, as soon as
daylight appeared, we moved on to the vicinity of
Round Top and formed in line of battle.   Here the
32d was detailed to form a skirmish line, to protect
the extreme flank of the army.   Colonel Prescott,

however, requested that the Regiment be excused from this duty, for the reason that it had had no experience, and but little instruction in skirmishing. The 9th Massachusetts was substituted, fortunately for them, and unfortunately for us, for as matters turned out, they were not engaged, and did not lose a single man during the fight of that day.

We remained inactive for a number of hours, the men providing themselves with food, and seeking the rest so much required. Officers and men laid down under the shelter of a ledge, and entirely oblivious to the roaring of the cannon and the bursting shell that passed over our heads, slept the sleep of the weary. It was the last sleep on earth to some of our number; to others a blessed boon, enabling them to endure the exhaustion and pain occasioned by wounds received at a later hour. It was nearly 3 o'clock in the afternoon before our repose was disturbed by orders to move forward.

Following the general design of these pages, to relate only the story of our own Regiment and what occurred in its presence, to paint only the pictures that we saw, there are yet necessary, concerning the battle of Gettysburg, a few words of more general description.

There had been several days of occasional contact between the hostile armies; each was concentrating its scattered corps, and meanwhile manœuvring to secure a favorable position for the inevitable battle. On the 1st of July the fighting had been heavy, and when we joined, the forces on each side were arrayed for a decisive contest.

Seminary Ridge, which was occupied by the Confederates, and Cemetery Ridge, which was selected for the Federal position, may be called parallel ranges of highlands. Between the two the country is not a mere valley sloping from the ridges to a common centre, but it is broken by knolls and swells of land which, like the ridges, are lower to the northward (our right) and more rough and broken toward the south.

General Sickles, with the 3d Corps, had, upon his own responsibility, advanced his line so that it occupied, not Cemetery Ridge, as General Meade had intended, but the broken swells of land lying between the ridges; and this advance of the left corps of Meade's lines, forming a salient angle, led to its being selected for the main attack by Lee.

The line of the Union army was irregularly curved, the right bending sharply back and resting on Rock Creek, and the left bowed slightly to the rear.

Between the positions here and at Antietam, there were many points of likeness, but the relative situation of the combatants was reversed. This time it was Lee's army that attacked, while to us fell the advantage of the defensive attitude and of the interior lines, by which reinforcements could speedily be moved from left to right or right to left, as the pressure of emergencies required.

As has already been stated, the 5th Corps was held in reserve during the early part of the 2d of July, and its position was such that by reason of the irregularities of the ground and the frequent patches of woodlands, we could see but little of our own lines, and of the enemy's nothing except the smoke of his batteries on Seminary Ridge.

The attack of Longstreet's corps, although bravely resisted, was too much for Sickles, in his unfortunate position, to withstand, and the immediate cause of our orders to move forward was the break made by the enemy in the lines of his corps. Our line of battle was hastily formed on the westerly slope of a hill, at the foot of which was the bed of a small stream then almost dry.

The division line was, because of the broken character of the hillside, exceedingly irregular, and walls and ledges were made useful for defence.

We were hardly established in our position, such as it was, before the attack came, the enemy piling down in great numbers from the opposite slope and covering themselves partially under the hither bank of the little stream. They were received by a galling fire from the division and driven back from our immediate front with great loss into the wood from whence they came. The men loaded and fired with great rapidity, some using much judgment and coolness, making every shot tell in the enemy's ranks; others, as is usually the case, excited and firing almost at random.

It was during this part of the fight that Lieutenant Barrows, an officer esteemed by all, was instantly killed. And here too, before the enemy was repulsed, many of our men were killed or wounded.

Further to the right the Union soldiers were not so
successful, and another break in our lines from the
enemy's charges compelled the command to fall
back, which we did in splendid order, carrying with
us our dead and wounded.   Moving to the rear and
left of its first position, the brigade formed in a piece
of woods bordering upon the wheat-field, which is
pointed out to visitors as the spot where were
enacted some of the bloodiest scenes in the battle of
Gettysburg.   This field was surrounded by a stone
wall, and when we first saw it, was covered with
waving grain.   Forming in line of battle our
brigade advanced across this field, taking position
in rear of the stone wall facing the enemy's lines.
On the right was the 4th Michigan, the 62d Pennsylvania holding the centre, with the 32d Massachusetts on the left.   The right of the 4th Michigan
rested near a wood or clumps of thick bushes where
it should have connected with the left of the 1st
Brigade, but by some mistake, either on the part of
the general commanding the division, or the officer
in command of the 1st Brigade, that body did not
advance as far as the 2d, but halted, leaving a large
gap in the line of the division.   Between the two
brigades was also a steep ravine leading up from
the "Devil's Den," a deep hollow in our front.

We were hardly in position here before the
attack came again, and the battle waxed hot and
furious.   We had been engaged but a short time
when Colonel Prescott, supported by two men, went
to the Lieutenant Colonel and turned over to him the

command of the Regiment, declaring that he was
wounded, and must leave the field.   The men
received the fire of the enemy with great coolness,
and returned it with spirit and success.   During all
this time we had seen nothing of our brigade commander (Colonel Sweitzer), and Lieutenant Colonel
Hull, of the 62d Pennsylvania, while in search of
him, informed Colonel Stephenson of the want of connection with our troops on the right, urging that something should be done at once or we should be flanked
there.   Upon the suggestion that Colonel Jeffers,
of the 4th Michigan, should change front and meet
the threatened danger, he hastened to communicate
with that officer, but before the movement could be
made, the blow came.   The enemy moving quietly
up the ravine charged directly upon the flank of the
4th Michigan, curling it and the 62d Pennsylvania
up like a worm at the touch of fire, and throwing
them into the greatest confusion.   Taking the order
from an aide-de-camp of the brigade commander,
who is always supposed to have authority to give
such commands, the 32d was falling back in good
order, when, for the first time, we saw our brigadier,
who, rushing from the woods, rode before the lines,
ordering the 32d to halt, demanding, with an oath,
to know why the Regiment was retreating.   Indig-
nantly replying that the Regiment was falling back
under orders from his staff officer, the Lieutenant
Colonel ordered the men to face about and stand
their ground.   It was a fatal mistake, and one which
caused the loss of many brave men.   For a few

minutes we stood; the enemy on our front, right flank, and nearly in our rear, pouring in a terrible fire, which the men returned almost with desperation, until we were again ordered to fall back, which we did, fighting our way inch by inch, rebels and Union men inextricably mingled, until we reached the shelter of the woods.

Just at this moment Colonel Stephenson fell, shot through the face, and Colonel Prescott who appears not to have been wounded at all, soon after again took the command.

The Pennsylvania reserves were forming for a charge. With a shout and a yell they fell upon the now disorganized ranks of the enemy and drove them like a flock of sheep for a long distance, almost without opposition. The 32d reformed and advanced again to the stonewall where they remained undisturbed, for their part in the battle of Gettysburg was ended.

The whole of this terrible fight was fraught with incidents, some grave and touching, and some even humorous. One gallant officer having discharged the contents of his pistol at the foe, at last threw the pistol itself at the head of a rebel. Another, wounded and faint sat down behind a large boulder. Two rebel soldiers tried to take him prisoner; then commenced a race around the rock; all ran the same way and he managed to elude them and escape. Probably not a soldier could be found who could not tell some curious incident which came to his knowledge during this fight. It was nearly sundown before the battle was ended for the. day. We must have been engaged three hours, yet so great was the excitement and so little did we mark the passing minutes that it seemed to have occupied less time than has been taken to tell the story. The 32d carried two hundred and twenty seven men into the action and lost eighty one in killed, wounded, and missing, among whom was Lieutant Barrows killed, and Colonel Stephenson, Captains Dana, Taft, Lieutenants Steele, Lauriat, and Bowers, wounded. The 4th Michigan and 62d Pennsylvania, besides their killed and wounded, lost nearly one hundred men prisoners, and also lost their colors. Colonel Jeffers of the 4th Michigan, probably the only man who was killed by the bayonet during the battle of Gettysburg, died in defence of his flag.

The frantic assault by General Lee oñ the 3d of July, fell entirely upon the right and center of the Union army, and the left was not attacked.

Colonel Stephenson gives this vivid description of his experience, one of those sad ones that attend a soldier's life among the wounded in the rear.

"On the 3d of July the wounded of the 5th corps were taken from the barns and other buildings in the immediate vicinity of the battle field, where they had heen placed during the progress of the fight, to a large grove about two miles distant.

The trains containing hospital supplies and tents had not arrived, and the wounded were placed under little shelter-tents, such as the soldiers carried with them upon the march. We lay on the bare

ground without even straw for our beds, and he who
obtained a knapsack for a pillow deemed himself
fortunate.

Just at night the attendants brought to the place
where I was lying, a young soldier of the 32d and
laid him beside me.   It was Charles Ward of Newton.   I remembered him well as one of the youngest
of the Regiment, one whose purity of character,
and attention to duty had won the esteem and love
of all who knew him.   The attendants placed him
in the tent, furnished us with canteens of water, and
left us for the night, for alas, there were thousands
of wounded men to be cared for, and but little time
could be spared for any one.   My young com-
panion had been wounded by a ball passing through
his lungs, and it was with difficulty he could breathe
while lying down.   To relieve him, I laid flat on
my back, putting up my knees, against which he
leaned in a sitting posture.   All night long we
remained in this position, and a painful weary night
it was.   At intervals we would catch a few moments
of sleep; then waking, wet our wounds with water
from the canteens, try to converse, and then again
to sleep.   So we wore away the night, longing for
the light to come.

No one came near us; we heard far away the dropping fire of musketry on the picket lines, the occasional booming of the cannon, and the groans wrung
from the lips of hundreds of wounded men around
us.   My young friend knew that he must die; never
again to hear the familiar voices of home, never to

feel a mother's kiss, away from brothers, sisters, and friends ; yet as we talked he told me that he did not for a moment regret the course he had taken in enlisting in the war of the Union, but that he was ready, willing to die, contented in the thought that his life was given in the performance of his duty to his country."

XII.

AFTER GETTYSBURG.

THE day succeeding the battle, we left Gettysburg in pursuit of the defeated enemy, followed closely by the 6th Corps, by way of Emmetsburg, Adamsville, and Middletown to Williamsport. Much of this time it rained heavily and the roads were. bad, but we had the good spirits which attend success, and were cheery, as became victors. Near Williamsport we encountered the enemy, and on the 11th and 12th of July pressed him back toward the river, but he succeeded in crossing the Potomac without further serious loss.

Perhaps the finest thing that the army ever saw was the movement forward in line of battle near Williamsport and Hagerstown. As far as the eye could reach on either hand were broad open fields of grain with here and there little woods, the ground being undulating but not broken, and we were formed in close column of division by brigade, the 3d Corps touching our left and the 6th Corps our right; and so we advanced across the wide, yellow fields in two dense lines which extended apparently to the horizon. This movement was continued on two successive days.

Then we tried a flank movement by our left, crossed the Potomac on the 17th, near Berlin, and keeping east of the Blue Ridge, were at Manassas Gap on the 23d, and stood spectators of some pretty fighting done by the 3d Corps, who secured possession of the pass. On the 26th we were at Warrenton, and remained there until August 8th, when we moved to Beverly Ford, and encamped there for five weeks.

Sergeant Spalding, in a letter home, describes our camp there as the cosiest he ever saw : "Our camp is in a forest of young pines, planted since our arrival. It looks beautifully, especially in the evening. I went out a little way from our camp last evening to take a bird's-eye view of it. How cosy it looked with the lights from our tallow candles glimmering through the trees from nearly every tent, which seemed almost buried in the green foliage that surrounded it. Our camp is laid out in streets, one for each company. At the head of each street is the captain's tent, which is surrounded by an artificial evergreen hedge with an arched entrance, with some device in evergreen wrought into or suspended from the arch — as, for instance, Company K has a Maltese Cross (our corps badge). Company I, of Charlestown, has the Bunker Hill Monument. Company D, of Gloucester (fishermen), has an anchor, &c., &c. But our tented cities, be they ever so comfortable and attractive, are short-lived. We build them up to-day and pull them down to-morrow. We may be quietly enjoying our quarters to-day, and to-morrow be twenty-five miles away. Such is a soldier's life."

ᵢ On the 12th October, 1862, General Porter ordered our Colonel to detail one company for detached service as guard to the reserve artillery of the army, and Company C (Captain Fuller) was detailed. When the detail was made it was supposed that it would be only for a few weeks, but they did their duty so acceptably as to result in being separated from the Regiment for more than ten months.

It was their duty to accompany the trains of the artillery reserve on the march, the men being distributed along the whole column and on each side of it, and they furnished the sentinels about the ammunition and supply trains, when parked for the night.

The duty was not very severe, and their position was one of comparative independence. It was pleasant to hear that a company of ours received praises alike from every commander of the reserve, and from the families of the Virginia farmers whose premises they had occasion to occupy. Their route was the general route of the army, and at Gettysburg they were under sharp fire on the 3d of July, when Lee made his last assault, but the total of their casualties, while absent from the Regiment, was small.

They brought back many recollections of pleasant camps and stirring scenes, and the story of their experiences brought a welcome freshness to the gossip of the battalion. They rejoined the Regiment near Beverly Ford, August 24th, 1863.

M

While we were encamped at Beverly Ford five deserters were tried, convicted, and sentenced to be shot, and the sentence was executed near our camp in the presence of the corps, massed on a hillside facing the place of execution. No more solemn scene was witnessed in the army than the march of those five men from the barn in which they had been confined to the graves in which they were to lie. They were dressed alike, in white shirts, trousers, shoes and stockings, and caps. The order of procession was as follows : First, the band, playing the death march, then four soldiers bearing an empty coffin, which was followed by the prisoner who was soon to occupy it, guarded by four soldiers, two in front with reversed arms, and two behind with trailed arms. Then another coffin and another prisoner, borne and guarded as described above, and so the five doomed men marched across the field to their graves, where each, seated upon his coffin, was to pay the penalty of desertion by death. Although at first they marched with firm and steady step, yet they staggered ere they reached the spot where they were to face death at the hands of comrades. Eighty men selected from the provost guard were there in line, posted to fire the fatal volley. When all was ready, the men having been placed in position and blindfolded, the officer in command of the guard, without a word, but by the motion of his sword, indicated the ready—aim—fire, and instantly every gun (forty loaded with blank and forty with ball cartridge) was discharged and all was over. Silently we viewed the solemn spectacle, and as silently returned to camp—not with cheerful martial airs, as when a faithful soldier, having met a soldier's death, is left to his last repose, but with the sad ceremony uneffaced, and all deeply impressed with the ignominy of such an end.

On the 15th of September we broke up this pretty camp and moved along to Culpepper, with some lively skirmishing, and then rested for another month with some picket duty but no warring.

A French Canadian who left without permission on our march to Gettysburg, and took to bounty-jumping for a living, was detected, returned to us, and at this camp was tried, sentenced, and punished for his offences in the presence of the entire brigade.

In the middle of a square formed by the troops who had been his fellows, one half of his head was shaven close, and his shoulder was branded with a letter D. The square was then deployed—the line formed with open ranks, the front rank faced to the rear, and the poor wretch, under guard, was marched down the path thus lined with on-looking soldiers, the musicians leading the way playing the Rogue's March, and then he was sent from the lines as not worthy to associate with an honest soldiery.*

Here, too, we received a reinforcement of 180 drafted men, who were assigned to the different companies, and of whom we made good soldiers.

---

*The scoundrel's own description of the proceedings was: " they shave my head — they burn my back — they march me in review."

Between the 10th of October and the 29th of
November the Army of the Potomac and the
Army of Virginia were waltzing about the country
between Culpepper and Fairfax. Frequently it
was "forward and back," sometimes "forward all,"
and occasionally "back to back." Generals Meade
and Lee called the figures, and we danced to the
music of artillery and rifles. There was in fact no
fun in all this; the campaigning was severe, and
some of the engagements were marked by sharp
fighting, but the campaign was mainly one of
manœuvres.

Sunday morning, November 29th, found our corps
in position, in the centre of the line of battle at
Mine Run, with orders to be ready to charge the
enemy's works at a given hour, when a signal gun
was to be fired. There the two great armies of
Viginia were brought face to face, each occupying
a strong natural position, about a mile apart, with a
deep valley between, through which passed a small
stream called Mine Run.

We have said that each army occupied a strong
natural position. The Confederate army however,
had us at a great disadvantage. They knew it and
expressed it by acts which spoke louder than words
— coming out from behind their works by hundreds
in the open field, seemingly to challenge us to
charge across the valley, which they knew—and so
did we—would be to many of our number the valley
of death. For we had to charge down the hill
across the Run and up the opposite slope, in the

face of a hundred guns, planted so as to sweep the field with grape and canister the moment we came within range, and thousands of muskets in the hands of the enemy, who were evidently not only ready, but anxious to see us storm their position, that they might mow us down like grass.

Before taking our place in the line we were ordered to remove our knapsacks and all needless baggage that might interfere with our movements when the charge was ordered. That was the time that tried our nerves. The field was before us. The obstacles to be met and overcome we could see, and with our past experience it was evident to all that the contemplated movement if executed must involve a fearful sacrifice of life on our side. For hours we watched, and waited in suspense the signal that was to open the conflict, and the relief we experienced when the order to charge was countermanded, can better be imagined than described.

At dark we retired a little way from our position in the line of battle, built our camp fires, cooked our supper, and laid down to rest. About midnight we were aroused, and falling into line moved to the right about a mile, where our corps joined the 6th corps which occupied a position in the woods, and there we formed in line of battle. The following day will long be remembered by us on account of our bitter conflict with Jack Frost instead of Johnnie Reb. The day was extremely cold, freezing the water in our canteens, and although in danger of freezing ourselves, we were ordered not to build fires, or in any way make ourselves conspicuous, for we were within range of the enemy's guns. Our situation was one of exposure and peril, for if we obeyed orders we were sure to perish with the cold, and if we disobeyed, as sure to draw the enemy's fire, with the risk of losing life or limb. We took the latter risk—built fires by which to warm ourselves, or chased each other in a circle around a tree or stump to keep our blood in circulation and our limbs from freezing. And when a solid shot or a fragment of a shell came whizzing through the woods where we lay, we hugged the ground more closely, or sought the shelter of some rock or stump or tree, until the firing ceased, then resumed our exercise, or gathered around the fire again to cook our coffee, warm ourselves, and make another target for the enemy.

Thus for three days and nights the two great armies of Virginia menaced each other across the valley of Mine Run. At last the movement was abandoned and the campaign ended by the withdrawal of our army to the north of the Rappahannock, and two days afterward we found ourselves in what proved to be our winter quarters at Liberty.

While in winter quarters we had the pleasure of seeing several ladies about the cantonments, among them Mrs. Faxon, the young wife of our surgeon, whose experience and memories of the time it may be better to render in the first person.

XIII.

A LADY AT WINTER QUARTERS.

EARLY in the winter of 1864, the 32d was in winter cantonments at Liberty, near Bealton Station, on the Orange & Alexandria railroad. Of course somebody must have commanded the army, but whoever he was, he never called upon me, and is of no consequence to my story. My orders to join came from an officer much more important in my eyes—the surgeon of the 32d, who, queerly enough, was also my husband.

After all manner of experiences I arrived at Bealton Station, a locality which by daylight appeared to be a quarter-section of Virginia land and a small, rough, and inconvenient platform of planks; but it was evening when I arrived—yes, a dark, rainy, December evening. A shadowy form having the voice of our garrulous quartermaster waited to welcome me, and by it I was ushered into the damp darkness, out of which loomed, by and by, the hazy form of an ambulance and two hazy mules—and then, but beyond and more misty, the upper half of what seemed to be my husband, and the ears of his horse. Whether I was sufficiently hearty in my greeting I do not know—I am afraid not, for all this was not what I had imagined would be my first impressions on coming within army lines.

My idea of an army was made up of brilliant sights and stirring sounds. Nice clean flags— bright-buttoned uniforms—flying horses and full bands of music, were essential parts of the picture which my fancy had painted, and here was nothing but wet and darkness and mud. Through mud a foot deep, the creaking of the vehicle and "soh" of the feet of the wading mules, only breaking the moist silence—I was driven to the mansion in which my husband was quartered, and which was to be my home for the winter. Out of all this dreariness, however, I stepped into the cheerful light of glowing windows, and was welcomed to a most hospitable wood fire, in front of which was a table set out with a smoking supper of tempting odor—and my surgeon appeared no longer misty and uncorporeal, but solid humanity, and looking really quite bright in the eyes, and happy in my coming.

The hearty welcome, the bright light, and the cheering warmth soon obliterated all memory of the weary journey and the dismal night. The fatted chicken had been killed for me, and was served with hot potatoes, corn-bread, tea, and cold meat. A bright little negro girl waited upon me, and it added to the pleasant novelty of my position to be served by a piece even so small of the "peculiar institution."

The "mansion" consisted of four rooms, the two on the lower floor separated by a hall; the kitchen was a small building across the yard—earth floored —and it was not only kitchen but bed-room for the black servants, who, however, did not seem to use any beds.   But all this I did not learn until daylight came again, and the drums, fifes, and bugles bursting out into reveille woke me amid dreams of home-life to the consciousness of my surroundings.   Listening to that stirring music (how exhilarating even now is the bare memory of the reveille) and looking out from my window upon the camp of our Regiment and of many other regiments, seeing everywhere the signs of real service, I was more than satisfied, and no longer bewailed the absence of my ideal army.

This winter was one of halcyon days to me. Accustomed to the rigors of a Northern winter, the many bright warm days of the season, in Virginia, were peculiarly enjoyable.   The country had been stripped of fences, and our horseback rides were limited only by our picket lines.   Now we walked our horses through the woods, the dry underbrush crackling beneath their hoofs—now cantered freely over some wide expanse of old fields,—reining up to pass some ugly bit of corduroy road, or to ford a full water-course.   In the foreground might be a "mansion," occupied by some general officer as his headquarters, or a group of negro huts still tenanted by blacks of all ages.   In the distance the high hills of the Blue Ridge, and perhaps between, in the middle distance, picturesque camps of artillery, cavalry, or infantry.

A few of the houses were still occupied by the families of their owners, among whom we made acquaintances; the able-bodied men were all "away," the women said; where,—they never told.

Besides our almost daily rides, we paid and received visits, and exchanged rather limited hospitalities. Quartermaster Hoyt entertained us frequently, and although his *piece de résistance* was invariably a dish of fish balls, yet having a cook who knew how to make good ones, his fare always seemed sumptuous. Once we dined with Colonel Prescott, who flared out with a joint of roast beef, but this was exceptional grandeur.

Our quarters became quite the evening resort for officers of the 32d, and the few ladies who were there, and the hours passed pleasantly away with chat and games and jokes and stories. I could not then with any success assume a matronly role, and sometimes perhaps actually enjoyed the practical jokes which abounded in the camp. Then, too, where ladies are but few, they certainly are better appreciated than in the crowded halls of fashion, and it was pleasant (for I am human and woman) to be the attraction in a circle of young and brave men.

Please don't anybody think that my time was entirely taken up with pleasures or trifling occupations. Even doctors need all manner of work done for them by their wives—there were some housekeeping cares, and the regimental hospital was none the worse for having a woman's eye over it. My first experience in dressmaking was in behalf of Mrs. O., a native neighbor, who had been useful, and possibly earned a trifle by mending for officers and men. To be sure when it was done it appeared that I had made the back of the basque all in one piece, without any seam, but that may be the fashion some day. No, I was not idle, and all days were not bright and happy, but the bright ones linger longest in my memory.

I did, once in a while, wish that in my peaceful life there might be mingled, just for seasoning, a trifle of real war; but one evening, when we were attending a dance over at the spacious log camp of Martin's battery, there came an orderly all splashed with mud, with news that a raiding party of the enemy was close at hand, and the party scattered, infantry officers hurrying back to their regiments, and all to their posts. The brass guns, which, decked in fresh evergreen, had formed quite a striking decoration to the temporary ball-room, were hustled away into position. The voices which had been saying pretty things to us changed to tones of command, hardly softening to tell us that safety forbade our return to quarters. Some sort of a hole was prepared for our safe-keeping in case of attack, but when all was quiet, beds were made in the log house assigned to us ladies, of boughs laid on raised boards, on which we slept soundly until daylight came, when the alarm was over, and it was safe for us to ride home. It was very nice for once, but my ambition for stirring scenes was fully satisfied.

Late in the season there was quite a grand ball, and on St. Patrick's day a merry party gathered to witness the games, races, and sports which had been organized by the officers of the 9th Massachusetts Regiment in honor of the festival. This was the height of the winter's gaiety; with the milder air of spring, we non-combatants must flit away to our homes, and leave our soldiers alone to meet the stern realities of the coming campaign.

But there were stern realities too, for us at home, as we waited, sometimes in dread, because we heard nothing, and yet again trembling for fear that we should hear a more dread *something*—trying even, while oppressed thus with terror and anxiety, to compose cheerful letters to the dear ones out of sight under the war-cloud. Is it wonderful that we welcomed with something of a weird satisfaction every call in behalf of the soldiers for our time, our labor, and our energy, or that we plunged into the work of our own sphere with a certain reckless desire to drown out in stirring occupation, the care and anxiety which haunted each idle hour.

Can anyone realize in these peaceful days what was one of the chief of women's sorrows then — that very often that which was the cause of their deepest grief and affliction, might be the occasion for public and general rejoicing, and that the wife of yesterday, the widow of today, must don her weeds of mourning at the moment when the country clad itself in gay bunting, and threw rockets to the sky for very joy that out of bloodshed there had come victory.

XIV.

AT LIBERTY.

DURING the winter of 1863-4, the portion of the Army of the Potomac which included our Regiment was encamped in a position to defend the railroad between Bealton and Warrenton, from attacks by guerillas, and the camp of the 32d was in close proximity to the village of Liberty, a very small place whose name meant, before the war, liberty to the white man only, and but for the "little unpleasantness" and its results, the name would have had no significance to men of color.

Liberty proved to be an agrecable camp for the 32d, for their rows of tented dwellings were pitched on a pleasant wooded slope where the ground was dry, with good drainage, an abundant supply of water near at hand, and soil less inclined to mud than in the greater part of the old Commonwealth of Virginia.

The picket duty was severe, as at this point there was a thoroughfare leading directly into the country of the enemy, and a railroad bridge, the loss of which would cause great annoyance to our own army by interrupting our line of communication, and cutting off one portion from its base of supply. But

there was much to enliven us and break the
monotony of camp life.

It was a little past midnight on the evening of the
dance which was so rudely interrupted, that the
long roll was sounded and, in scarcely more time
than is necessary to write it, the Regiment was
under arms and deployed in various directions for
the protection of the camp. The disturbance was
caused by a squad of rebel cavalry who had forced
the picket line at a weak point, their presumable
object being a raid on the United States paymaster,
who came into camp that night to pay off the brigade ;
but the yankee soldier generally keeps picket with
eyes and ears open, and whoever would cross his
beat must have a feather tread. The paymaster
(the late Major Holman), although the object of
the attack, slept quietly through the whole uproar,
and did not wake until morning. Apparently his
safe might have been stolen and carried off without
his being aware of it. We were out about two
hours, when the enemy having been driven beyond
our lines, we were sent back to our quarters.

An amusing incident occurred here one dark night
which created quite a sensation on the picket line,
at that time under command of Captain Farnsworth.
Going the rounds at two o'clock A. M., posts eight,
nine, and ten were found on the *qui vive*. They
were stationed in the edge of a wood, where just
across a narrow strip of grass-land there was another
belt of forest. For some little time they had heard
footsteps and other sounds which led them to believe

that their posts were being reconnoitered by the enemy. After waiting some minutes and leaving orders that no aggressive movement should be made, but that in case any party should be seen to leave the opposite wood, the sentinels should order "halt," and if not obeyed should fire, the captain passed on his tour of inspection. Before the round was completed he heard a shot from this direction, succeeded by perfect quiet, and when again at post nine the sentinel reported that he had done as directed, that some object had, in spite of his challenge, continued to approach, that he had fired and dropped the intruder, who or which, upon examination, proved to be a *mule*. Well, he ought to have halted.

It was from this camp that a night expedition was sent after deserters. Outside our lines, at distances varying from two to four miles, were several dwelling houses occupied by families for whose protection it was common to billet a man on the premises as a " safeguard." Such men were not subject to capture on this neutral ground, and their posts were very desirable, as they were well cared for by those under their guardianship, and had little to do, plenty of leisure, and often very pleasant society. But there were troubles connected with such arrangements. The men in camp hearing of the attractions of these places so near at hand where coffee, salt, and other supplies were exceeding scarce, and where gifts of them were acknowledged by various favors—were tempted to slip over the lines, each with little parcels saved from his abundant rations, supplemented, perhaps, with a spare jackknife and a few needles, to seek adventures among the natives. The fact that they ran the risk of capture and imprisonment probably added zest to such escapades, but was of itself a good reason why they should be prevented. In fact, it was within this very territory that Major Edmunds and his orderly were captured.

At the roll call at retreat, March 31st, 1864, it appeared that several men were "unaccounted for," and there was little doubt as to the cause of their absence. The colonel, who had previously considered the propriety of some action on his part, was now at the end of his patience, and determined to put a check upon the practice. Sending for an officer who was at that time serving on a general court martial, and consequently not considered "for duty" in the Regiment, he told him of his wishes and offered him the command of the detachment which should make a detour through a portion of the neutral territory, and search for and, if possible, capture the missing men.

A detail of twenty-eight men was finally made from nearly twice that number who volunteered for the duty. Included in this number was one man who had been on safeguard duty in the neighborhood that we proposed to visit, and who could act as a guide to the party.

The party were in light marching order, each man with a day's rations and forty rounds of ammunition in the cartridge boxes, and it left camp an hour and a half before midnight, at which hour it was intended to reach the house of Colonel N——. The path was a narrow forest roadway, and for the greater part of the distance led through what was known as the " three-mile wood." The night was moonless and very dark, and the detachment filed on, mile after mile, always on the alert and suspicious of every sound, until at last, and in good time, they reached the cleared land about Colonel N.'s " palatial mansion." Deploying an advance guard they proceeded with the utmost caution to surround the house, and but for the dogs, who challenged loudly, the purpose would have been readily accomplished; but the inmates were speedily astir, alarmed by the baying of the hounds, and lights danced about from window to window. Whether rebel soldiers were among the occupants or not could not be told, but soon men came out at the doors, and their footsteps could be heard as they ran, but no one could see ten feet away to distinguish a man from a tree.

Orders had been given not to fire without command, and to give chase in the darkness would risk the loss of men without any good result. The party therefore went on cautiously to surround the house, and men were posted in such manner as to command all approaches to the mansion, with orders to halt and arrest whoever attempted to enter or to leave. After these guards were posted, the remainder, under a sergeant, were marched away for a half mile up the road, making considerable noise as they went, and then halted to await orders. In the meantime

N

the squad about the house was kept quiet in the
darkness, out of the way of any light from the windows.   After ten minutes had elapsed the door of
the mansion was opened and some one looked out,
thinking, no doubt, that the disturbers were well
away.   Then, as if the door opening had been a
signal, the sound of footsteps was heard approaching
slowly through the dry leaves and twigs in the woods ;
then a whispered conversation, and again the steps
approached. A moment later two men came on, until,
when within five feet of the commander, they were
halted with the order, " Surrender, or I fire."   At
first they turned, evidently with the intention of
escaping, but changed their minds, saying, " Don't
fire, we surrender."   These proved to be two of the
men of whom the expedition was in search.   They
had been in the house, and had started at the alarm,
thinking that the troops were from the rebel lines ;
had waited until, as they supposed, the detachment
had passed on its way, and then were going back to
the house.   Leaving these men under guard the
house itself was summoned.   The door being opened
by a woman, and the lady of the house called for,
four of the party entered and were referred to a
beautiful and accomplished young lady of perhaps
twenty years.   Miss N. received them courteously,
but declared upon her honor that no men from our
camp had been in the house that day or evening.
She was informed as politely as possible that there
was an error in this statement—that two such men
had already been secured, and that search would be

made for more. This resulted in the arrest of a third man, and having bagged him and apologized for the disturbance that had been caused, the party moved away.

"While life lasts," says the captain, who commanded, "I shall not forget the flash of the young lady's eyes when I questioned her assertion. I have often thought that if every southern soldier had to look for approval or disapproval into such a pair of eyes, it was no wonder victory often perched on their banners when the odds were against them."

At half past two in the morning the party was back again in camp with three prisoners, and found that two others who ran from the house had returned of their own accord. All of these were of course technically deserters, but none were severely punished. The result of this expedition was to put a stop to a practice by means of which valuable information, no doubt, reached the enemy.

XV.

OUT ON PICKET.

PICKET duty may be the most agreeable or it may be the most disagreeable of all the duties of a soldier, but it is always an important, and is often a dangerous one.

Picket-guards are formed by details on orders from headquarters. Sometimes the guard will include the entire regiment, or details from several regiments, but if the orders are from the battalion headquarters, it is usually composed of detachments from several companies. The officers are detailed from the adjutant's roster and the designation of the enlisted men from each company devolves upon the first or orderly sergeants. The officers, non-commissioned officers and men, are supposed to be taken for duty in rotation, and woe befall the unfortunate orderly who designates one of the confirmed growlers out of what he considers his turn, as laid down on his own time-table, and many are the threats heaped on the head of the sergeants, which happily are never executed.

Under command of the ranking officer, the detachment is marched out and posted to guard the line assigned to its protection — usually there is

merely a chain of sentinels who are relieved at regular intervals of time from the main body; but
sometimes, and always in the case of detached outposts, the men are divided into groups of three or
more, under the supervision of the non-commissioned officers of the guard, while the commander
of the whole line establishes reserves at points convenient for reinforcing it in case of need, and
assigns to the subalterns the command of various
portions.

Relieved from the wearisome round of camp
duties and parades, and placed where each man has
his own responsibilities, and must exercise his own
judgment, picket duty often becomes an acceptable
change, both for officers and men. In the warm
season the men make a sort of picnic of their tour,
and out on the front edge of the occupying army
they can frequently obtain articles of food, which,
although common enough in civil life, are real luxuries to those who have been limited in their diet to
the rations issued in the army. They bask in the
sunshine, or loiter in the shade—and when it is
their turn for repose, the jacknives are busy and the
chat is lively.

Sometimes our picket-line would be on a river,
the opposite bank of which was guarded by the
enemy, and there would be times of unofficial truce
when we traded over the stream coffee for tobacco,
etc., and when we even made visits to each other,
and talked as freely as if we might not at a
moment's notice be enemies again.

But it is one of the unfortunate facts in a soldier's life, that picket duty is not confined to quiet times or pleasant weather. The growlers usually maintained that it was always stormy when they were out on picket, and in three winters that we dwelt in tents within the boundaries of Virginia, there were many rough times on the picket lines when the rain poured down continuously, saturating the ground, clinging to the grass in the open, and to the undergrowth in the forests, and streaming down from the boughs — wet, wet — water, water, everywhere; on the ground where we slept, on the stone or log which was the only seat; dribbling through a corner of the tent, usually down the neck of its occupant, or making a little rill off one's overcoat and into one's boot top.

Or perhaps it was snow or sleet that stung our faces and chilled us to the marrow; or perhaps, worst of all, the clear cold of winter which our little picket fires, when they were permitted, did but little to overcome.

There was one occasion while we were at Liberty, on which we were indulged with all of these in turn. It was early in the spring of '64, the day had been warm and rainy, unseasonably warm and quite seasonably rainy, the rain continuing into the night and the wind rising to a gale that made all manner of noises in the wood in which our line was posted. The men all soaked through, had hard work to keep their ammunition dry and their rifles in condition for use, and all of us, uncomfortable as mortals

could be, feeling as if the night would never pass
and morning never come, wished more heartily than
ever "that this cruel war was over," that we might
have a chance to get in out of the rain.

All of a sudden the wind shifted to the northwest,
and we had first hail, then snow, and finally clear
cold weather, the gale all the time continuing; the
men themselves, almost chilled to icicles, were soon
clothed in armor of ice, which cracked and rustled
as they tramped along their beat, beneath a clear
sky and stars that shone with winter brilliancy.

The morning came at last, and with the rising sun
there was exhibited one of those marvels of beauty
which can come only from such a preparation.
Every twig and branch of tree or shrub, and every
spear of grass or tuft of herbage clad in a coating
of ice, blazed with the hue of the rainbow. The
trees in the forest seemed loaded with jewels, and
the meadows were strewn with them.

But the power of the spring sunshine dissolved
the gorgeous display, and thawed out the sentinels
from their encasements of ice; the wind ceased,
the mildness of the balmy Southern spring returned,
and soon from every man a cloud of steam rose in
the quiet air, and as their clothing dried and their
bodies warmed, the spirits of the men thawed out,
and they who, in the previous twenty-four hours,
had passed through various stages of discomfort,
were cheerily chaffing one another as they made
their breakfast of hot coffee and soaked cakes of
what had once been hard-tack, and very likely wrote

home the next day about the charms of the Southern climate, which gave them such delicious spring weather in what was at home the winter month of March.

Whether it is summer or winter, hot or cold, sunshine or rain, day or night, and however peaceful or stormy the scene may be, the picket guard must keep their eyes open and their powder dry. Constituting the outposts of an army which trusts to them, they must be always alert against surprise. And although we may have been accustomed for weeks to exchange friendly civilities with the pickets over the river, the time would come when each would do his best to kill the other. When some change was contemplated, or some movement began which it was desirable to conceal from our adversary, orders would be sent to the pickets to open fire on those of the enemy.

Such orders were of course first notified to the other side, and no advantage was taken by either of existing truce relations. After that warning, whoever showed out of cover was a target for the enemy's picket, and frequently no fires were allowed, because the light or smoke would aid the aim of the foe.

If the movement was a direct advance from our front, the first order would be announced by shouts of "Look out, Johnnie, we're coming," and some shots sent purposely in the air, and then came the driving in of the enemy's pickets.

Or possibly the boot was on the other leg and it was we that were driven in, in which case it was our duty to cause all possible delay to the attacking force. The reserves were added to the line, and as we fell back the whole would be relieved by other troops sent forward at the alarm and interposed between us and the rebels, whereupon we were marched to join our respective regiments and companies.

Sometimes it is desirable to capture some men from the pickets of the opposing army, in order or in hopes of obtaining information, and sometimes a picket is captured for a lark, or because of a favorable chance — a chance which generally implies neglect of duty on the part of the captured men.

In one instance an outpost party of five men, believing themselves to be at a safe distance from the enemy, ventured to indulge in the luxury of a game of cards, for which purpose they placed their arms in a stack, and soon became deeply interested in the game, from which they were aroused by a summons to surrender. Upon looking up they discovered a single man of the enemy, standing between them and the stack, his rifle trained on the group, and himself so posted as that he could supply himself with their rifles after discharging his own. Thus he could put two or three of his opponents *hors de combat*, while, all unarmed, they could not possibly harm him ; and so the five surrendered to the one, who marched them before him to his own lines.

When things were lively on the picket lines and the men alert, it was wearing business. The strain of constant watchfulness, especially at night, peering into the gloom and imagining that you see forms or hear movements—the knowledge that your own life may depend upon the keenness of your vision—the fear of mistaking friend for foe—the need of quick intelligence and rapid reasoning—all make up an exhausting kind of duty.

At one such time, one of our officers, a brave fellow, but one whose experience of picket duty was insufficient, thinking to ascertain the origin of suspicious sounds outside our lines, went out on a scout, expecting to return at the point where he left, but mistaking his way in the night, he came upon our chain of pickets at another post which he had neglected to warn of his doings. As he continued to approach when challenged, the sentinel fired, and next day among the casualties reported was, "One officer wounded on the picket line, arm, severely." No one was to blame but himself.

That same night the men, nervous from the frequent firing along the line, one of the posts became aware of the sound of steps out in the bush field on their front, evidently approaching nearer and nearer; then one of the men could see what seemed to be a man crouching near the earth and creeping through the brush with frequent hesitation; finally the sentinel challenged, and receiving no reply, fired. The crack of his rifle was followed by the agonizing grunts and dying squeals of a stray Southern porker who had yielded up his life for the lost cause.

It may be that accidents of this last type were more frequent than was necessary (there were three pigs killed that night), but vigilance on the part of the guards is always praiseworthy, and the orders against marauding could not apply to such a case, even if the result was a good supply of fresh pork-chops along the picket lines next day.

XVI.

ON FURLOUGH.

IN the winter of 1863-4, the great majority of the men of the 32d reënlisted for a term of three years, under an order which in such cases gave the entire reënlisting body a furlough of thirty days. It was only after much struggling with bumbledom that everything was smoothed out and the furlough granted, so that the Regiment could return as one body.

Leaving the camp and the remainder of the men under command of Captain Fuller of Company C, the Regiment left for Massachusetts to enjoy its vacation. It was a little before noon on Sunday, the 17th of January, 1864, a bright and mild winter day, that we arrived in Boston, and our first impression upon arrival was that all the people of Boston were gathered about the Old Colony station, but there were enough of them left to line the whole route through the city, as we marched first to the State House to pay our respects to Governor Andrew, and as we moved thence to Faneuil Hall, where a bounteous collation awaited us. Notwithstanding the day the troops were saluted along the line by the cheers of the people, and the salvos of artillery.

At Faneuil Hall, after all had been satisfied with
the repast, Governor Andrew arose to address them
and was greeted with hearty cheers. He spoke in
substance as follows :

Soldiers : — In the name and in behalf of the Commonwealth and of the people of Massachusetts, I greet your
return once more to your homes and to the soil of the
venerable Bay State. The cordial voices of the people
who have welcomed your procession through the streets
of Boston, these waving banners, these booming cannon
breaking the stillness of our Sabbath day with voices
echoing the sounds of battle — all, all bid you welcome —
welcome home. The grateful hospitality of Boston
beneath the venerable arches of Faneuil Hall welcomes you.
Our hearts, speaking the eloquence of affection, admiration, and pride no words of mortal lips can utter, with
beating throbs bid you welcome. Hail then, soldiers of
our cause, returning for brief relaxation from the toils, the
conflicts, the perils of war, hail to your homes. Here let
the war-worn soldier-boy rest for a while, and rejuvenate
his spirits, refresh his heart, and re-erect his frame. Here,
too, I trust, shall your ranks be filled by fresh recruits of
brave and patriotic hearts, imitating your zeal, vieing with
your courage, and following your example. I cannot,
soldiers of the Union Army, by words, by eloquence of
speech, in fitting measure repeat your praise. This
battle flag, riddled with shot and torn with shell, is more
eloquent than human voice, more speaking than language,
more inspiring, more pathetic than music or song. This
banner tells what you have done ; it reveals what you
have borne. And it shall be preserved so long as the last
thread remains, so long as time shall leave a splinter
of its staff — a memorial of your heroism, your patriotism and your valor.

While I greet the return of these brave and stalwart
men to the homes of Massachusetts, I remember those comrades in arms whose forms you have left behind. Yielding to the shock of battle, many of those brave soldier-boys
to whom, in behalf of the Commonwealth, I bade farewell

some months ago, fighting for that flag, defending the rights and honor of our common country, maintaining the liberties of her people, the traditions of the fathers, and the rights of humanity — have been laid low.   They sleep beneath the sod that covers the rude grave of the soldier. Oh, rest in peace, ye hero martyrs, until the resurrection summons shall call you to that other *Home!*   No longer obedient to any earthly voice or any human leader, you have made your last report, and in the spirit have already ascended to join the Great Commander!   The humblest soldiers who have given their lives away, will be remembered so long as our country shall preseve a history.   Their fame will be acknowledged with grateful affection when ten thousand prouder names shall have been forgot.

> " While thousand as absurd as I,
> Cling to their skirts, they still shall fly,
> And spring to immortality."

I give you praise from the bottom of a grateful heart, in behalf of a grateful and patriotic people, for all that you have suffered and for all that you have attempted. And now on this holy sabbath day, let us remember with the filial thankfulness of sons, with the devoted piety of Christians, as well as the exulting confidence of patriots what the *God of our fathers* has done for us, from the beginning.   Unto *Him* and not unto us be all the praise and the glory.   Unto Him who sitteth upon the throne and ruleth the nations let us give everlasting ascriptions of praise, that through the trials of many a defeat, through the despondency of many a temporary repulse, our arms have been conducted to many a triumph, and our minds to still loftier heights of moral victory.   You are fighting now for the cause of your country, and also — for Washington used to love to declare he drew his sword — "for the rights of human nature."   And now let all of us, living men, on this holy day and on this sacred spot where our fathers were wont to meet in the dark hours of earlier history — let all of us living men, consecrate ourselves anew, by the vows of a new obedience, to our country, to humanity, and to God.

At the hall the Regiment was dismissed, but only to meet renewed evidences of cordial hospitality. Company I was entertained the same day by the civic authorities of Charlestown, and Company K the next day at Newton. The officers breakfasted with Colonel Parker at the Parker House on Monday, and on the 16th of February, on the eve of their return, dined with him at the Revere House, on which latter occasion Governor Andrew was present and expressed, as no one could do more more heartily or more genially, his appreciation of the past service of the Regiment, and his good wishes for their future.

Besides these there were balls and dinners and entertainments to occupy all the time that the soldiers were willing to spare from their home enjoyments, until their departure February 17th, and on the Monday ensuing the Regiment was again in camp at Liberty, with its new title of "Veteran," which the 32d was the first, from Massachusetts, to assume.

XVII.

THE WILDERNESS CAMPAIGN.

WHEN one of the many interviewers of President Lincoln introduced the subject of the election of his successor, the President is reported to have declared, with his wonted quaintness of expression, that "it wasn't a good plan to swap horses while crossing a stream," by which he was understood to argue in favor of his own reëlection.

Unfortunately he limited in practice the force of this pithy saying to his own office and his own continuance therein. He showed little hesitation in "swapping" one general for another, and often selected the middle of a very rapid stream as the place for the swap.

The last of these changes—that which placed General Grant in command of all the armies in place of Halleck—was certainly no injury to the service. Perhaps the greatest mistake of all, in a military point of view, was that which took General McClellan from the same position. It was the long-continued service of Lee which made him what he proved to be—the ablest of the Confederate generals. Such a mistake as he made in attacking Meade at Gettysburg would, or should have, proved the ruin of any Union general.

208

But at last we had generals who had come to stay, and Grant's obstinate pluck, assisted by Meade's tactical ability, well supported by the political powers at Washington, were to give us final success.

April 30th, 1864, we broke camp at Liberty, and with the army led by our new General-in-Chief Grant, advanced to meet the enemy. The first day's march was only five miles. Our division, gathering near Rappahannock Station, encamped for the night. The next morning we crossed the river for the fifteenth time, making another short march to Brandy Station.

May 3d we marched leisurely to Culpepper (distance six miles), and halted there several hours. Marched all the night following, crossing the Rapidan at Germania Ford at eight o'clock in the morning, where we halted for breakfast. During the day we pushed steadily forward into the Wilderness, marching till dark, when we bivouacked near Wilderness Tavern, in close proximity to the enemy.

May 5th.— Early in the morning we were in line of battle, with orders to fortify our position. We had an abundance of material with which to build breastworks, and axes, spades, and picks were freely used by willing hands. In a few hours we built a formidable line of defense, behind which we expected to fight, but were disappointed (as we had often been before) when the order " forward " was sounded. About noon we advanced, leaving our entrenched position for other troops to occupy. Our

o

division, which had the honor of opening the campaign, moved cautiously forward to attack the enemy. Soon we encountered their skirmishers and drove them back to their lines. As we approached the enemy the Regiment made quick time in crossing a road along which poured a shower of grape and canister. Scarcely had we reached the shelter of the woods on the opposite side of this road when we came under fire of infantry, who gave us a warm reception, but were pushed back before our steady advance to their second line, where we engaged them until dark.

In this our first engagement in the Wilderness campaign our Regiment suffered little, owing to the favorable lay of the ground over which we advanced. We lost none killed, and but thirteen wounded.

That night we lay on our arms. There was, however, but little chance for sleep, as we were in the extreme front, and almost within speaking distance of the enemy. Early the following morning the fighting was renewed on our right and left, and was then very severe. The rattle of musketry and the roar of artillery, as it reverberated through the forest, was terrific. Although we were under the fire of artillery, with the din of battle thundering in our ears, many of us slept, unable longer to resist nature's demand for repose.

A pine tree standing just in the rear of our line of battle was severed about midway by a cannon ball, and the top fell to the ground and stood there erect beside the trunk.

Towards midnight we were suddenly withdrawn, and after marching (or rather stumbling) through the woods in the darkness for about a mile, we halted near where we were on the morning of the 5th. There we laid down our arms and unconditionally surrendered to an overwhelming force —" nature's sweet restorer, balmy sleep."

As it was quite dark when we arrived, we did not know that a twelve-pound battery was in position behind us and only a few rods distant, until about daylight, when it opened fire and brought us to our feet in quick time. The occasion was quickly ascertained. The enemy had assumed the offensive, and was advancing in force against our works. They were handsomely repulsed, however, and with this exception we were not disturbed that day. Several times the enemy shelled us, but being protected by breastworks, we suffered no loss. The line behind us was less fortunate, several shells exploding there, killing and wounding a number of men. Thus we passed the third day of the battle of the Wilderness.

At night the location of both armies was plainly indicated by blazing camp-fires, as well as by the cheers of the *Yanks* and the yells of the *Rebs* — demonstrations that were intended by each to blind the other in regard to their contemplated movements.

About nine o'clock we began our first flank movement towards Richmond. Neither tongue nor pen would do justice to our experience of night marches such as this. All night we marched and halted (but halted more than we marched). We did not often stop to rest, but jogged along at a snail-like pace. When our column moved we marched route step, arms at will, and when it halted we came to order arms and leaned upon our guns, keeping our places in the ranks, so as to be on the alert to prevent a suprise, ready for any emergency.

About midnight we had just emerged from the woods and, halting in the road, stood leaning on our guns. It has been said that soldiers can sleep while marching. Whether this be so or not, it is certain that at this time three quarters of the men were three quarters asleep, and the other quarter more so, as we waited there for the column to start.

At this moment the troops ahead came suddenly to the front to meet, as they supposed, an attack of the enemy in ambush, which proved to be only a squad of stragglers who had stolen away into the bushes by the roadside, and turned in for a good night's rest, but had been awakened at our approach. The sudden alarm created a panic which ran like an electric flash through the entire column, sweeping the soldiers from the road as quickly and effectually as though a battalion of cavalry had charged upon us unawares. Lieutenant-Colonel Stephenson was on his horse, but availed himself of the momentary halt to drop off into a gentle slumber. Suddenly he was awakened to find his horse whirling around and himself apparently alone.

Our double-quick movement in the dark from the road to cover effectually awakened us, and we resumed our places in line, to laugh over our experience and continue our tramp till daylight, when we halted near Spottsylvania. One would suppose that we needed rest and sleep by that time, but instead of that our Regiment was ordered to support a battery, and we remained during the day (Sunday), spending most of the time fortifying the position. There was considerable fighting during the day, and at its close we moved to a new line of battle, which we occupied during the 9th, 10th, and 11th of May. This was within easy rifle range from the enemy, and being able only partially to protect ourselves behind the breastworks, several casualties occurred in the Regiment.

Sergeant Spalding was hit in the neck by a spent ball, which he carefully saved. A man by his side was struck in the forehead by a bullet which knocked off his hat, made an ugly scalp wound, and finally left him stunned and bleeding; the first symptoms of his revival were a hand outstretched and a " Good-bye, boys," to those around him; but he soon recovered enough to go to the rear for repairs.

On the morning of the 11th, General Grant sent to Washington that memorable dispatch which was characteristic of our leader and meant success, although at a terrible sacrifice of life, limb and treasure: " We have ended the sixth day of heavy fighting, and expect to fight it out on this line if it takes all summer."

Captain Dana had been on detached service, acting as aide-de-camp to General Dana, who was in command somewhere out West. Having obtained a leave of absence of sixty days he returned to the Regiment, which he joined here in the Wilderness, and resumed command of his company. Early in the campaign he " captured " a wooden chair from some house as we passed, which he persistently carried wherever he went. At every halt the captain brought his chair to the ground and sat himself down in it comfortably and complacently. In every fight his "private chair," as he called it, shared his dangers and rode upon his shoulder. In one of our scrimmages a rifle shot struck the chair, and the captain returned, among his casualties that day as wounded, " Private Chair in the leg—badly."

The 12th of May, 1864, is a date never to be forgotten by any of the 32d who were present in the attack on Laurel Hill that day. Brief as was the action, the loss of the Regiment in proportion to the numbers engaged, was greater than in any battle of the war.

That morning found us where we had been for two or three days, in front of Laurel Hill, and distant hardly more than a quarter of a mile from the works of the enemy. Between us and them were two swells of land, which afforded us some protection from the enemy's missiles. The summit of one of these was occupied by our pickets, and the other by the pickets of the rebels.

About nine o'clock A. M. we received orders to attack the position of the enemy on Laurel Hill, and the brigade, commanded by Colonel Prescott, advanced with a rush across the intervening space.

As the line of battle started, it overran the picket line—dashed down the little depression in their front, over the next rise of ground, but at the foot of Laurel Hill the men, whose momentum had carried them thus far, faltered under the terrible fire, and laid down within a short distance of the enemy's line of works. Here the ground did not cover the left of the Regiment, and while Colonel Stephenson was trying to draw his left under shelter, he saw that the regiment on his right had broken and was falling back in great disorder, and at once ordered the men to save themselves.

The advance had been disastrous, but as usual the retreat was far more so. In the 32d five bearers fell before the colors reached the old position behind our works; of the 190 men who advanced in the regimental line, 103 were killed or wounded, and from the time that they left the works until the remnant had returned, less than thirty minutes had elapsed. Among our wounded were Lieutenants Lauriat, Hudson, and Farnsworth, Adjutant Kingsbury, and Captains Bancroft and Hamilton; the latter of whom died two months later of his wounds.

From that day until the 23d, the Regiment was almost constantly in position in front of the enemy at Spottsylvania Court House and other localities, the service varied by repeated change of location all in the direction of the left, the building of new breastworks, picket duty, etc.

At the commencement of the war, the shovel was derided by a considerable portion of the people of the North, and even by the inexperienced and over-reckless men in the army, but the soldiers of the Army of the Potomac learned from experience the value and advantage of the utensil. After long and weary marches, the tired soldiers, if placed in positions confronting the enemy, would almost invariably, and often without orders, throw up earthworks before they wrapped themselves in their blankets for sleep.

On the morning of the 23d we resumed our march in the direction of the North Anna River, Crawford's division of our corps, which was composed almost entirely of Pennsylvania troops, taking the advance.

Our destination was Jericho Ford on the North Anna. When within a mile or two of the ford, at a fork in the road, General Cawford by mistake took the wrong way, and had advanced some distance in that direction before his error was discovered. Without waiting for that division to countermarch, General Warren, our corps commander, directed General Griffin with his division to cross the ford. Our brigade took the advance and forded the stream, which was about four feet deep. Reforming at once upon a plain, the brigade advanced in line of battle into a piece of woods, preceded by the 22d Massachusetts as skirmishers, under the command of Major Burt, one of the most skilful officers in command of a skirmish line in the army. We had barely entered the woods when our skirmishers drew the fire from the enemy's picket line, and the bullets came whistling over our heads quite freely.

The enemy soon fell back, and after gaining some ground we were directed to fell trees and erect another line of works. The men worked with great zeal, but had not finished when the enemy came upon us in full force, General Hill's corps essaying to drive us from our position into the river. The attack fell upon our division, which received the impetuous charge with a steady fire, and the enemy retired. Yet, notwithstanding the merciless reception which was given them, the Confederates pushed forward again about 5 P. M., and finally the line of the 9th Massachusetts broke under the pressure, rendering our position critical. The enemy poured through the interval, thus endangering our whole line; but their headlong course was checked by a well-directed fire from a battery hastily placed in position, and served under the eye of General Warren.

Unable to sustain this raking fire of canister, the Confederates gave way, and our line was reformed and strengthened. During this time the 32d, which formed the left flank of our battle line, maintained a continuous fire, the men loading and discharging their rifles with great rapidity. It is impossible to tell how long this action was in progress, as in the excitement of battle one can make but little note of the passage of time, but after a sharp, quick struggle, which seemed to last but a few minutes, and yet probably consumed more than an hour's time, the enemy withdrew, baffled in his attempt to force our position.

If such a thing could well be, this was the most enjoyable fight in which we participated during the

pounding process we were obliged to undergo from
the Wilderness to Petersburg. It was the only
engagement in which we had the advantage of
remaining under the cover of our works and receiving the attack of the enemy. In every other action
during this campaign these conditions were reversed,
and our comparatively trifling loss demonstrated the
disadvantage under which we had habitually been
placed.

This engagement proved that the enemy was on
our front in force, that he had again divined his
adversary's plan of flanking his army, and that any
further advance in this direction must be gained by
hard fighting. We remained in our position during
the night, receiving no further annoyance from
the enemy. The next day we were moved to the
right, and on the 25th again moved a short distance
in the direction of Hanover Junction, where we
threw up works and did picket duty until nightfall of the 26th, when we received orders to retire,
which we did silently, leaving our pickets to face the
enemy until the army had recrossed the North
Anna. Our division crossed at Quarles' Ford, and
marched all night and the next day in the direction
of the Pamunkey River.

After leaving the North Anna our next encounter
with the enemy was in the vicinity of Mechanics-
ville. On the morning of the 30th our brigade
advanced in line of battle through the Tolopotomy
Swamp, driving the enemy's skirmish line, which
made but little resistance, until we came to open

fields around Shady Grove Church, where we found him in force, protected by earthworks. This advance through the woods was very toilsome ; briars, fallen trees, and similar obstructions impeding our progress, made it difficult to preserve the line of battle. Many of the men were badly shod ; some had no covering for the feet, yet were compelled to march over briars and stumps which abounded.

The men had started on the campaign well provided with shoes—not new, perhaps, but in good condition—and twenty-five days' constant service, in rain and sun, dust and mud, had left them in a pitiable condition. Yet there was no help for it, no supplies upon which to draw, for it was the 6th of June before we saw our baggage and supply trains. During this period of thirty days, neither men nor officers could obtain any change of clothing ; the best that could be done was to catch a few hours, while at rest, for washing, wait for the sun to do the drying, and meantime go without.

During the afternoon there was considerable desultory firing, and our loss for the day amounted to twenty-one killed or wounded, among them Lieutenant George W. Bibby, killed.

About midnight we were relieved by a brigade of the 9th Corps, and went into camp. June 1st and 2d we were in the reserve, but on the 3d were aroused before daybreak to take part in the battle of Cold Harbor.

Our part consisted of a charge across an open field under a severe fire of grape and canister. We drove the enemy out of one line of earthworks and into another, where he made a stand. The real battle of Cold Harbor, probably, did not occupy more than twenty minutes. It was the same along the whole line as with us—a rapid charge under a galling fire from the enemy, who, protected by earthworks of great strength, easily repelled our attacks. Our brigade was, perhaps, as successful as any, for we did drive the enemy from his most advanced position, but he retired to one of greater strength. This attack was made before five o'clock in the morning. During the remainder of the day we laid quiet, within the redoubt we had captured, the enemy occupying his interior line not more than two hundred yards away. We kept up a constant fire, watching for every man who had the courage to show himself, thus hindering as far as was possible the working of the Confederate guns. The defences on our front were well constructed, and evidently laid out under the supervision of an experienced engineer. Indeed we learned from a prisoner that they were begun two weeks before we reached the place, by order of General Lee, who, it appears, foresaw that General Grant would necessarily be brought to this point if he continued " to fight it out on that line."

Between the lines of works occupied by our brigade and the enemy, the ground was covered with pine-trees felled and slashed across each other, making the passage through exceedingly difficult for troops, even had they been unopposed. But, in addition, the enemy had posted a battery in such a position that he could sweep the field with the fire of his guns, from which there was no shelter.

In view of all this we were not much elated when we received an order that at six o'clock P. M. we were to attack the enemy in our front, without regard to the movements of the troops on either flank. Lieutenant-Colonel Stephenson, believing that, under the circumstances, the movement could not be successful, sent to General Griffin, the division commander, a description and sketch of the position of the enemy and the ground before us, whereupon the order was so changed that we were not to advance until the 9th Corps, which joined our right, should move. It can be imagined how anxiously we watched the movements of the 9th, but the hour came, and the artillery signal for the charge was unnoticed by the troops on our right, who did not budge, and we were glad indeed when darkness came on and we knew that we had, at least for the time, escaped the terrible ordeal we had expected. We know now that the order to charge was given to the commanders of every corps, but was disregarded by every one; feeling that, after the experiences of the morning, another charge would result in fearful loss of life, with no effect upon the enemy's position. Our loss during the day was ten killed and twenty-one wounded. The loss to the Union army was over thirteen thousand killed and wounded; that of the Confederates, less than one thousand.

For a few days after the battle of Cold Harbor there seemed to be an intention on the part of General Grant to commence siege operations. We were then about twelve miles from Richmond, and on the same ground where, nearly two years before, was fought the action of Gaines' Mill — the first of McClellan's seven days' battle in 1862. The prospect of another campaign in the swamps of the Chickahominy was not attractive, and no regrets were expressed when on the 12th of June, General Grant abandoned his attempt to attack Richmond directly, and headed his columns for the James River.

To cover this change of plan, the 5th Corps crossed the Chickahominy at Long Bridge, and threatened to force a passage through White Oak Swamp, but as soon as the rest of the army had crossed the James, we took up our march southward, and followed to a point a little below Wilcox Landing, where we were ferried over the river, and on the 16th the whole army was on the right bank preparing for a new campaign.

XVIII.

THE BOMB PROOFS.

AFTER the long marches of the spring campaign of 1864, through the Wilderness to
Spottsylvania Court House, across the North Anna,
through the Tolopotomy Swamp to Bethesda Church,
thence *via* the Chickahominy, White Oak Swamp,
and Charles City Court House to the James River,
the 32d Regiment crossed the James and marched
to a point on the Norfolk Railroad, about three
miles from Petersburg, where, on the 18th of
June, they took part in the charge which drove
the enemy into their last line of intrenchments.
It was in this action that Colonel George L. Prescott fell, mortally wounded. While the engagement was not an entire success, it gave us the
vantage ground of the crest of a hill, which we
retained, and whereon we established our line of
entrenchments ; and this was the position from
which the Burnside mine was afterwards made and
exploded. After this line was established, our
Brigade was ordered to the rear, into camp along
the Jerusalem plank road, where we were held as
reserves for special duty ; and this was not, as might
be supposed, light duty, for while there we were

busy day and night, building a large earthwork fort, which was named Fort Prescott in honor of our colonel. Here Lieutenant-Colonel Stephenson, suffering from his wounds, resigned and left us, to return to civil life, and Major Edmunds was appointed Colonel, Captain Cunningham, Lieutenant Colonel, and Captain Shepard, Major.

On the 12th of July, after being in reserve somewhat over three weeks, during which we had been called upon twice to reinforce the 2d and 6th Corps lines, we were ordered into the trenches, and began our life in the bomb proofs. Our first term of service there extended from July 12th to August 16th, a continuous period of five weeks, and must have been experienced to be fully realized.

In order to give the reader an idea of what a bomb proof is, we will describe the method of its construction. First, a hole is dug in the ground, which, of necessity, when in front of an active enemy, must be done under cover of darkness; this hole is perhaps four or five feet deep, providing the ground is not too wet; then the top is roofed over with logs of wood held up by cross timbers; then the earth which has been dug out is thrown over the logs, which makes the whole comparatively watertight and proof against solid shot or shells, such as the enemy seemed to delight in tossing over into our lines in season and out of season, giving us frequent surprises and placing some of us *hors du combat*. There were, of course, openings to these subterranean caverns so that those who were to occupy them could crawl in and out. The openings were usually not much larger than was needed for a man comfortably to get in and out, and had an adjustable log to cover the major portion of the aperture, so arranged that it could be moved on and off at pleasure. This entrance was left on the side opposite the enemy, so that direct shots could not penetrate it, the only danger on that side being from shells exploded among the bomb proofs casting their fragments through the doorways into our underground domiciles. This would, after all, occasionally occur, sometimes arousing a sleeping soldier with a summons to another world. If one could choose the ground where he would locate such an underground mansion, he might make it a dry and comfortable abode, and one that would be comparatively healthy; but the ground assigned to the 32d was a clay soil, rather springy, where in many places two feet of excavation brought us to water, therefore a part of the domicile had to be above ground; and this was protected by inclined timbers, built like a lean-to, with a palisade front to make it proof against the ordinary shot and shell.

There were many exciting scenes and occurrences among the bomb proofs. Occasionally, in the middle of the night, a solid shot or a shell would come singing through the air and pounce down on one of the huts where half-a-dozen soldiers were dozing away, and the shock would startle them so that for a short time they would hardly know whether it was an earthquake or an attack by the enemy, but

P

finding that the roof had not fallen in, and seeing no danger at hand, they would usually turn over and resume their slumbers.

Within these huts we were obliged to pass our time when off duty and, as would be naturally expected, they proved a fruitful source of sickness.

Many of our men, delirious with malarial fever, were sent from the bomb proofs to the hospital, where they were dosed, first with a medicine composed largely of spirits of turpentine, next with strong acids, and then with quinine and spirituous liquors. If there is anything that will take the conceit out of a man in a short space of time, it is this malarial fever when it gets a good hold. It is wonderfully tenacious in its grip when once it does get hold, leaving the strong man when it must, but never leaving the weak man while the breath of life remains in him.

On Saturday the 30th of July, the Burnside mine as it was called, was exploded, but the result was hardly what had been hoped and expected. There was indeed a great panic among the enemy, but the advance obtained for our lines was inconsiderable, and the fear of similar incidents was not confined to the rebel troops. Men thought and some spoke of possible counter-mines, and to the dangers of war which had become in some degree familiar, there was now added another and an unpleasant possiblity —of an irresistible explosion from beneath; one which bayonets could not repel, and from which our bomb proofs could afford no protection. Confined to unhealthy caves when not exposed to more palpable dangers, deprived of opportunity for wholesome exercise and limited by the circumstances in the range of our diet, wearied by excitement and worn down by constant new alarms, it is no wonder that our numbers decreased nor that men were despondent.

Scarcely a day passed that some were not killed or wounded, and sickness was more effective than gunpowder in sending men to the rear or putting them out of the fight.

Our second tour of duty in the trenches was from the 1st to the 3d of September,—but it was in a drier place, and we suffered comparatively little.

Five weeks in the bomb proofs depleted the Regiment as much as any whole campaign in the field had done before, and it was with glad hearts that we received the order to give place to a relieving force.

Surgeon Faxon of the 32d was placed in command of the hospital of the 5th corps, near City Point, and when the army had settled down to the seige of Petersburg, Mrs. Faxon was ordered to the front, and a description of the hospital and of hospital life from her point of view will not be uninteresting.

XIX.

OUR CORPS HOSPITAL.

IT was a bright, warm, September afternoon in 1864, when the hospital transport, on which I was a passenger, loosed from the Seventh street landing in Washington and steamed away down the Potomac and out into Chesapeake Bay. So long as daylight lasted there were many objects of interest to occupy my eyes and thoughts, and when night closed in, finding that sleep would be an impossibility in the stifling heat of a state-room, I willingly resigned myself to the idea of passing the night on deck, for the sky was cloudless, and the full moon shone on the wide expanse of quiet waters.

The next afternoon we were steaming up the James River, under wooded banks, by neglected fields, past deserted plantations. Here and there might be seen some great homestead such as Carter's, which had escaped destruction, standing patriarchally among its negro quarters and numerous outbuildings, but even these few were evidently deserted and desolate.

About sunset, having passed Harrison's Landing, we seemed to be approaching some great mart of trade, so varied and bustling was the scene which

presented itself to us.   Beyond the masts and rig-
ging, and the smoke stacks and steam of the water
craft, were seen groups of tents, long ranges of
whitewashed barracks, log-huts and shanties of
every shape bearing the signs of sutlers and licensed
traders.   Among these were moving uniformed
soldiers and officers, on foot and mounted, negroes
driving mule teams, negroes leading mules or
driving ambulances drawn by mules, sentries on
duty and detachments relieving guard, and over all
flags flying gaily.   This was City Point, and such
the busy bustling life of the place which was the
base of supplies for the army.

Landing at a wooden pier, I and my luggage
were loaded into an ambulance.   Driving past General Grant's attractive quarters, by what must have
been pleasant homes, now occupied for army purposes, through what had been avenues of noble trees,
which were now rows of stumps, two miles over a
rough road brought me to the depot hospital of the
5th corps.

A broad drive-way led to the headquarters' tents,
in front of which a sentinel was on duty.   Three
hospital tents, each 15x17 feet, were arranged,
opening into each other, and furnished as office,
parlor, and bedroom.   In front was an arbor-like
enclosure made of green reversible blinds — probably borrowed from some "mansion" — which gave
to one inside an agreeable seclusion.   The furniture
consisting of sofa, chairs, tables, mantel, hanging
shelves, bureau, wardrobe, and washstand, was

made of soft, unpainted, unvarnished pine of rude construction. Cushions were made of army blankets, and the bed, with its linen counterpane and sheets looked tempting. The tents were floored and in each was an open fire-place with broad hearth-stone, which I hope did not come from the cemetery near by.

Dinner, an elaborate meal of several courses, was speedily served in a neighboring tent, and bore witness to what might be accomplished by culinary skill, combined with a few pans and a stove, in a space four feet square. We were hardly seated when, at what proved to be its accustomed hour, a band commenced to discourse a programme of excellent music. Thus cheerfully my life on the Appomatox began.

The broad drive by which I had entered the camp was the street upon which were quartered all the officers, the assistant surgeons occupying tents on the same line with ours and on each side.

At right angles to this were streets formed by the tents of the patients, nurses, and servants. The central street, directly opposite the headquarters, was wider than the others, and in the middle of it was the dispensary. Three tents, 15x17 each, opening one into another, extended from street to street. In each tent were six beds, by each of which a little table held basin and towel. Along the front of the tents were plank walks, and above on a framework of posts and rails were spread branches of trees to furnish shelter from the sun. Across the farther end of the streets were the mess tents, seven in number, supplied with tables, etc., for the meals of the convalescents. Beyond them was the diet kitchen, five tents, and behind them the quarters of the cooks. On one border of the hospital camp were the tents for the nurses (soldiers) and for the Sanitary Commission, and at the opposite extremity, under a group of persimmon trees, were accommodations for the military guard of one hundred men. In one corner was the property room — a log-house in which, carefully arranged, labelled, and registered, were the effects of those who died, and on the outer limit were the negro quarters, stables, etc.

In the rear of our street and parallel to it was another, through which a railroad track was laid, and there, after a battle, I have seen many car-loads of wounded men brought in, lying on the floors of rough cars, into which they had been loaded from the field of action. All grimy with the heat, dust and wounds of battle, they were placed upon stretchers, and by the convalescents and nurses were carried to the dainty beds. They were first washed and put to bed, then supplied with food and drink, then visited by the surgeons, assistants, and nurses.

The arrangements for cooking were, of course, upon a very large scale. Huge coppers were used for boiling, and brick ovens for baking. In one of the latter three barrels of beans could be cooked for the Sunday dinner.

A little Scotch woman, Miss Duncan, was in charge of this diet kitchen, having a number of men under her direction ; no time was frittered away, a perfect system was maintained, and the men submitted meekly to her despotic sway. I have seen a six-foot man rush for sand and mop, to erase an accidental spot of grease before it should be discovered by her sharp eyes. Everything under her *régime* was a miracle of neatness and economy. The pans were kept shining and arranged in regular order on the shelves, and the store-room was dazzlingly neat. The smallest number of rations issued from her kitchen was 5,000 per diem, and she has sent out as many as 15,000 in one day. Nothing was wasted ; the surgeon was bright enough to secure beef of the best quality, and even hoofs and tails supplied fine jelly and excellent soups, and what could not be used directly was sent to feed the swine at the piggery.

The negro camp was filled with families of contrabands who had found their way within our lines. These were served with rations, and drawn upon for such assistance as they were competent to give. The women washed for the hospital, and the men did all sorts of rough work. Sleeping from ten to thirty in one tent, they lived by day out of doors, and negroes of all ages and all colors basked in the sun or hugged the fires, or rolled about in the dirt. Many of the children came in with only one article of clothing, and that very commonly was a coffee bag with a hole for the head to go through. One old woman said that she came in because she had heard that " the champagne was a-goan to open." Rough as they fared to our eyes, it was evident they had never lived in such sybaritic luxury before.

Every part of the extensive camp was swept daily ; neatness was the order everywhere. The precision and beauty of the routine, and the exactness which followed discipline, spoiled me for civil life at home afterward, for I craved that system, punctuality, and order which cannot be found except under military rule.

Passing down the walks in front of the patients' tents, their thin white faces claimed one's pity, but there was comfort in seeing here, within hearing of the droning voice of the cannon and the tearing sound of musketry, that the victims of the battle found a quiet place to rest, where, lying in the soft air and bounteous sunlight, carefully nursed and daintily fed, their wounds might be healed and their ills abated before they were again to be plunged into the chaos of war.

In the winter many of the tents were replaced by log houses, and some of these became charming cottages, having many conveniences. Around my house was a little garden with a tiny fence, and oats were sown in the beds to form ornamented borders, in which all the corps badges were represented.

But with the spring all this was to disappear ; the army moving forward to final victory, and the *impedi-menta* like myself, going back to civil or civilized tameness in the cold North. But even now I have but to shut my eyes as my neighbor, the old army bugler, practices the calls in the clear winter air, and again returns the memory of those days.

XX.

ABOUT PETERSBURG.

SUCH portions of the army as were not stationed in the trenches were called upon frequently to repel attacks, and occasionally were sent out on expeditions to destroy railroads, or otherwise to interfere with the enemy's supplies, and to weaken his lines. One of these was the action on the Weldon railroad, August 18th, in which we lost thirteen men. Another led to the battle of Peeble's Farm, September 30th, 1864.

The expeditionary force was composed of the 5th and 9th Corps, and the movement was as usual off to the left. After marching three miles our brigade was in front of Fort McRea, and the men were ordered to lie down in the edge of a piece of woods until the remainder of the attacking force could be posted. The 32d Massachusetts was directly in front of the fort, the 4th Michigan on the right, and on the left a brigade of new troops, which however took no part in the attack.

It was about three o'clock in the afternoon when the order for the advance was given, and we moved out into an open field, finding ourselves, perhaps half a mile distant from the fort and the line of the

breastworks of the enemy. Their batteries opened
upon us promptly, but old soldiers know that it is
not the great guns that are most to be feared, and
our line moved steadily on until it came within rifle
range of the rebel works and the small arms began
their deadly work ; then the order for double quick
was given and the men, sure that the faster they
moved the less was their risk, dashed forward with
alacrity and in a few moments closed upon the lines
of the enemy. Colonel Edmands in this charge
was disabled by a wound in his leg below the knee.
Colonel Welch, of the 4th Michigan, while in the
act of urging his horse over the first defences, fell
mortally wounded upon the breastworks.

The first to mount the earthworks was a captain
of "ours" ; he stood long enough to swing his
sword above his head and shouted "come on
boys, we've got 'em"—then dropped inside closely
followed by two other officers ; one of them had
jumped the ditch and the other having jumped into
it, scrambled out with the assistance of his men.
When these three officers with one soldier mounted
the parapet, its defenders were still firing, but when
they were inside, the fort was captured. Surrounded by our troops, they knew that if four men
could get in in spite of them, the rest would follow,
and soldiers quickly learn to know when the day is
lost and to submit gracefully to the misfortune of
war. In the fort we made forty prisoners, of whom
eighteen were officers, and captured one piece of
artillery—minus the horses—which the gunners

managed to cut loose and run away, although not without a struggle.

As we gained these the first of their works, the enemy retired to his second line of defences and the prisoners being speedily secured, we pushed on with the rest to the attack. At the inner line there was some close work where bayonets and butts of rifles came into use, but there was no great resistance, for the enemy were badly demoralized and our chief interest centered in an effort to capture one of their colors. The bearer was a tall and vigorous man, but one of our comrades, a gallant young fellow, grappled the bearer and secured the flag. Just as he turned to escape with his prize, one of the rebels with a musket tripped our man, who fell, still clinging to the staff, but at the same moment the stalwart standard-bearer grasped the flag, broke the lance and bore away his flag, leaving the northman only the wrong end of the stick.

After carrying the second line, our division was halted and left resting on their arms while the 9th Corps passed into the front and followed the routed forces. They were however soon met by a force which proved too strong for them, and after a short struggle were in their turn driven backward, losing all that they had gained and threatening to cause confusion in the whole line, but our General (Griffin, called "old Griff" for short) seeing the danger and having unlimited faith in his command, threw the division into the pathway of the rebels, now flushed with hope of final victory, and with a few volleys checked them and turned the tide again ; darkness closed upon the fight and the field was ours. We called the battle that of Peeble's farm, because it was fought upon the lands of General and Colonel Peebles, two officers of the Confederate army. The fort was afterward named Fort Welch in honor of the gallant Colonel who had baptized it with his blood.

After the fort was captured and the men disarmed, the fight raged for a time along the line, and the Confederate prisoners huddled together under the breastworks for protection from the missiles which were still uncomfortably numerous, and which they had no further occasion to brave.

While thus situated, a large number of men of our brigade swarmed in at the entrance of the fort, and one of their officers, a captain of a Maine regiment, rushing up to a squad of the prisoners, pistol in hand, fired, shooting one of them in the head. It is charitable to presume that the captain was blinded with the excitement of the fight, but he narrowly escaped a similar fate himself before his brother officers hurried him away ; and it is likely he may never forget the shouts of opprobrium and the epithets of ignominy which the deed provoked from the Union men who witnessed his cowardly or reckless act.

When the battle commenced, and as we moved to the assault, the brigade of new troops which was posted on our left was deployed to protect that flank, and no doubt thought that their time had come. The roar of the battle was in their ears, and the sight of killed and maimed was before their eyes for the first time, and as is commonly the case with raw men at such times, they did not set much store on property ; and so finding themselves cumbered with well-crammed knapsacks and new and heavy overcoats, they threw them off to improve their fighting trim. As the veterans came out of the fight and saw such wealth scattered about, no doubt some of them seized the occasion to better themselves, by exchanging old for new, and for some days afterwards the new men were apt to claim as their own every new overcoat worn by any of our men; but in the army the fashions of dress are so similar that it is not easy to see any difference between one man's coat and another's, and so our Johnny Raws had to put their losses down to the debit of experience account and draw new clothing for that " lost in battle."

The experience of this day was a very cheering one to the troops engaged ; we had had our enemy "on the hip " and kept him trotting, and we felt that it might be what indeed it proved—the beginning of a chase which should tire him in the end.

The 9th Massachusetts Regiment did not reënlist, and when their three years' term of service expired, their reënlisted men and late recruits were transferred to the 32d. On the 26th of October the enlisted men of the 18th and 22d, whose time of service did not expire with that of their regiments, were also added to our battalion, increasing its numbers so largely as to require the organization of two

new companies, L and M, the officers for which
were transferred with the men.   Thus the Regiment
was now composed of twelve companies, and its
parades exhibited a front which two years before
would have been respectable for a brigade.

By general orders of October 26th, a reorganiza-
tion of our division was effected, by which we were
transferred to the third brigade, which was then
composed entirely of veteran regiments.

On the 6th of December, 1864, we were, as we
supposed, established in winter quarters, on the
Jerusalem plank road, in a dry and healthy location, when orders came for a movement, and we
regretfully abandoned our improvements and took
up a line of march along the plank road.

We marched three miles that afternoon and
bivouacked by the wayside.   The next morning,
early, we started again toward our destination, of
which we knew nothing, except that our haversack
rations meant three days of absence, and the forty
rounds in our cartridge boxes implied no expectation
of big fighting.   After marching twelve miles the
command was massed at the bank of the Nottoway
River, which we crossed about midnight and yet
moved on.   At daylight we were at Sussex Court
House, and at three in the afternoon reached what
proved to be our objective — the line of the Weldon
Railroad, five miles from Jarratt's Station.

Here we rested until dark, when the men were
ranged out along the railway and set to work to
destroy it.   First the rails were removed ; then the

sleepers were taken up, piled and fired; when the rails, laid across the burning ties, were heated so as to be pliable, they were doubled and twisted in such manner that they could not be relaid unless rerolled. Then the same operation was repeated on another length of track until several miles in all were ruined. It was a long day's work, and we bivouacked the second night along the road-bed, making our·coffee at the smouldering fires.

On the 10th we started on the return march, and although it was raining and very muddy, we made twenty miles that day, reaching a bivouac near Sussex Court House. The next day we passed over the Nottoway, and on the 12th reached the Jerusalem road, and went into camp within a half-mile of the spot we had left to make the excursion which has been described. Here again we built dug-outs and huts, in which we were allowed to remain until the early spring.

On the return march the men did considerable foraging on their own account. A goose, a chicken, a turkey or duck, seemed to be a part of the men's equipment. One squad captured a little pony, harnessed him to a sulky, and loaded the sulky with their knapsacks and live stock. One man appeared under a stove-pipe hat, but it didn't wear well. At night, sweet potatoes, sorghum molasses, and applejack, were abundant in the camp.

Our enlisted men were not apt to be damaged by the over-supply of spirituous liquors. The sale of them was strictly forbidden, and when a suttler was detected as implicated in the trade, his entire stock of all kinds of merchandise was confiscated, and in some cases distributed among the near-by soldiers.

Whiskey was used as a medicine, but its value as such is problematical. As a restorative for men exhausted by labor or by battle, it has, no doubt, a good effect, but it should not be given until the work is done or the battle fought. It would have been a great advantage to the army if the commissioned officers had not been able to obtain supplies, for Dutch courage is a poor substitute for the real thing, and a clear head is even more important to him who commands than to him who has only to obey.

On the Weldon Railroad expedition, some of the men, by a mysterious instinct, discovered several barrels of apple-jack which had been concealed under a stack of hay, and many of the canteens were filled with spirit by the soldiers as they passed. Several of these, overcome by their potations, fell out of the line of our outward march, and probably to sleep off the fumes, stretched themselves out upon the broad veranda of a planter's house. On the return march they were found there with their throats cut—dead—and the murder was avenged by the burning of the house. No doubt many more suffered for their excess by imprisonment in Southern barracoons.

The New Year of 1865 found the Regiment in log huts near the Jerusalem plank-road, a mile in the rear of our works before Petersburg, on swampy ground. The two wings of the battalion alternated in fatigue duty, building, extending, or strengthening works, the labor continuing day and night.

Suddenly on the afternoon of February 4, 1865, orders came to move the next morning (Sunday), at daylight. The general impression was that there was to be another raid on the railroad connections of the enemy, and the camp huts were left standing. At daylight on the 5th, the column started and sunset found us near to Nottoway Court House. We were ordered out on picket, but were recalled about midnight and marched until dawn, when we were at Hatcher's run—the point where that stream is crossed by the Vaughn road.

The day before, the 2d Corps had been engaged with the enemy here, and the 32d was posted in some rifle pits on the further side of the Run, out of which the rebel forces had been driven. Our Regiment was the extreme right of the 5th Corps, and on its right connected with the left of the 2d Corps across the stream. About 2 o'clock P. M., Crawford's division advanced from the left, moved across our front and encountered the enemy; two hours later our brigade was put in by General Warren to fill a gap in Crawford's line, and the contest was sharp until about dusk, when the onset of a fresh body of the enemy drove back Crawford's command in some confusion. The locality of the action was in a thick wood of pines where we could not see to any great distance, and as our part of the line held on, we found ourselves with the 155th Pennsylvania quite alone and flanked on both sides. It required considerable coolness and some sharp fighting to enable us to get back to the original line of battle, and our losses in doing so were heavy — 74 in killed, wounded, and missing; included in which number was Major Shepard, who was made prisoner while commanding the brigade line of skirmishers, and Captain Bowdlear severely wounded. The action we named that of Dabney's Mills.

Until the 11th we remained in the same position. The weather was very cold and stormy, and the enemy's artillery at times very annoying, but no infantry attack was made. On the 11th the corps changed its line slightly, and we soon had a camp more comfortable than that we left on the Jerusalem road. Here we remained digging and picketing until we started out on the final campaign.

In the action of the 6th, Major Shepard commanded the skirmish line in front of our brigade. When Crawford advanced across our front, the pickets became useless and the Major proceeded to call them in and to join the brigade. While marching to the left, as he supposed in the rear of the Union line of battle, he happened into the gap which had just been made in Crawford's command by a Confederate charge, and he suddenly found himself in the rear of the enemy; at the same moment he was struck in the head by a musket ball, which had just force enough to stretch him senseless on the ground. The Major recovered to find himself an object of interest to a half-dozen rebel stragglers, one of whom exchanged hats with him,

another borrowed his nice overcoat, while others
contented themselves with his various equipments.
Perhaps Shepard did not recover full consciousness
until the moment when one of the plunderers ordered him to take off and yield up his boots. But
this was the feather too much. Those boots were
new, elegant, and costly, and the Major made a
stand in and for them, replying to all threats by the
declaration that they couldn't have the boots, and
that he preferred death to the loss of them.

How the affair might have ended we cannot say,
had not an officer appeared in sight, to whom the
Major formally surrendered himself; but thereupon
the stragglers left him with his boots and his life to
boot, and both have given him much contentment
since that day.

XXI

THE LAST CAMPAIGN.

THE month of March is really a spring month in the latitude of southern Virginia, and out of the attending frosts and thaws, storms, mists, and bright days which make up the winter there, we had come to the time when the buds were breaking out into greenness, and when even within sound of the great guns, the venturesome birds would sing the lays of spring.

The whole army was inspired with the feeling that the last campaign was about to open, and that the triumph of the Union cause must be at hand.

For six weeks we had been established in our huts, when on the 29th day of March, early in the morning, we bade good-bye to our village camp, and with the 5th Corps moved out to the rear and left. The weather was warm and as the march proceeded, personal property in the way of clothing, which had been valuable in the winter season, and convenient in the camp, began to increase in weight and to decrease rapidly in value. As the men realized that we were off this time in earnest, they began to shed their surplus clothing. The roads were difficult and the march toilsome. At every

halt loads were lightened, and spare blankets, overcoats, shelters, etc., strewed the line of march, until
by nightfall all were in light marching trim.

In the absence of Colonel Edmunds, disabled by
sickness, and Major Shepard, prisoner of war,
the Regiment to the end of the campaign was
commanded by Lieutenant-Colonel Cunningham,
assisted by Captain Bancroft as acting major.

The direction of our march finally led us toward
the Boydtown plank-road, near which in the afternoon the 1st and 2d brigades of our division
became hotly engaged, and ours (the 3d,) was put
in position in a low, level, and swampy field. During
the night it set in to rain with that ease and abundance which seems to be characteristic of the climate,
and we passed a thoroughly uncomfortable night,
during which men thought regretfully of the
blankets and rubber sheets which they had thrown
away during the previous·day.

Through Thursday the 30th the rain continued,
but about noon the 32d was deployed in front as
skirmishers, with orders to feel for the enemy —
feeling for him in the sloppy weather, we found
him behind some log breastworks, from which
we rooted him out and pushed him a short distance backward. But the enemy in his turn got to
be pressing, and our ammunition becoming scarce,
we were in our turn pushed back to our starting
point. The Confederates even charged the line
of our corps, but were repulsed with considerable
loss.

Late in the afternoon, with replenished cartridge boxes, we reoccupied the log breastworks, and being ordered to feel forward again, did so. This time it was a fort and an open field with too much artillery for comfort, but we got up close, burrowed, and held on. It seems that we had reached around to the extreme right of Lee's line of works for the defence of Petersburg, and hereafter we were to be free of these inconvenient obstructions to our way.

Friday, March 31st, at 5 A. M., we were relieved by the 2d Corps, and moved off again to the left, where General Warren posted the divisions of his corps, in *cchclon* a little west of the Boyd-town road. The ground, owing to the long rain, was in a condition very unfavorable to any movement, and our formation was hardly completed when the 2d and 3d divisions, (Crawford's and Ayer's,) were attacked and driven back with some loss, but our division (the 1st,) held its position, and the 2d and 3d coming into line with us, the whole corps, preceded by a strong skirmish line, again advanced and pressed the rebels hard.

Captain Lauriat commanding four companies of the 32d was in the line of skirmishers, and seized the opportunity, as the lines closed, to draw off on the flank, and through a bit of wood got into the rear of the enemy's skirmishers and stampeded them. So rapid was our advance that at one spot we captured the enemy's dinner of bacon, as also a number of guns in stacks.

Our corps was now the extreme left of the Union army. Sheridan, with the cavalry, was farther to the left, but entirely detached ; he had been attacked and pretty roughly handled, and considerable alarm was felt for his safety. During the afternoon our brigade, under Colonel Pearson, of the 155th Pennsylvania, was sent out to the left to reconnoitre and, if possible, to reinforce Sheridan. Entirely surrounded by skirmishers the brigade moved off to the left, but, although constantly gaining ground, their movement was so retarded by the brisk resistance of the enemy's skirmishers, that it was dusk before he was driven over Gravelly Run, and the next morning we learned that Sheridan was all right.

April 1st, 1865. — Before eight o'clock this morning the 5th Corps was again in connection with the cavalry Corps, and both were placed under the orders of General Sheridan. In fact, for the ensuing eight days, we became a sort of foot cavalry—if there be any such arm known to the service.

It was afternoon before there seemed to be any real resistance to our onward progress, but then there was the sound of heavy firing in front, and we soon came upon what was to be the field of the battle of Five Forks. The cavalry, dismounted, were sharply prodding the enemy with artillery and carbines, and the 5th Corps was brought up and formed on their right, and pushed rapidly forward.

We found no enemy in our front, but soon discovered that we had passed beyond the line of his formation ; whereupon, by a wheel to the left and a rapid dash, we came in upon his flank and rear, surprising, overwhelming, and entirely routing his forces, more than one-half of whom were made prisoners. The fighting was sharp but short, and our success complete.

It is impossible to overrate the exhilaration of the men in and after this action. With small loss to themselves, they had taken four or five thousand prisoners, and the ground was strewn with the arms and equipments which the enemy had thrown away in his hasty attempt at flight. The feeling was general that now, at last, the superior numbers and power of the North were beginning to tell, the days of digging and burrowing were over, and the day of triumph near at hand.

That night, by order of General Sheridan, General Warren was relieved, and General Griffin (our "Old Griff") was placed in command of the 5th Corps. It is not easy to see what default in duty could have been ascribed to Warren, and it is probable that the real explanation of the change was merely Sheridan's preference or partiality for Griffin, who was patterned more after Sheridan's taste.

That night, too, Colonel Cunningham was placed in command of a brigade of skirmishers, consisting of one regiment from each brigade in the 1st Division, with orders to deploy them at eight o'clock the next morning, and advance directly west. The 32d was, of course, one of these regiments, and its command devolved upon Captain Bancroft.

April 2d, Sunday.—Promptly at eight o'clock, while the dull muttering of the great guns told us of the last struggle far away in front of Petersburg,

Cunningham deployed his brigade of skirmishers under the eye of General Sheridan, and we moved on, up hill and down dale, for the most part through a region covered with woods and but little inhabited.

Moving west, as ordered, we came at 11 A. M. to the South Side Railroad, where we captured a train filled with wounded and sick Confederates, and also gobbled up a large number of sound rebels and quantities of army stores, and then pressed on, still westward, for two miles farther.

From women and from our prisoners, information was obtained to the effect that the remains of two divisions of the enemy had passed in this direction on their retreat from Five Forks, and also that General Lee, with the Army of Virginia, was then moving out of Petersburg and heading towards the south ; and, indeed, we could plainly see the clouds of dust which marked their line of march.   This information was communicated to General Sheridan, but at 4 P. M. we were drawn back to the railroad and thence marched eight miles in the direction of Petersburg, and there bivouacked for the night.

The next five days were occupied in a most exciting chase.   Sheridan's command, consisting of the 5th Corps and the cavalry, entirely detached from the army, was hastening to bar Lee's line of retreat. On the 3d and 4th we marched twenty miles each day ; abandoned wagons, forges, guns, and caissons were seen quite frequently.   By our seizing the railway at Jettersville on the 4th, Lee lost the only railroad line by which his escape could be facilitated.   On the 8th we marched all the day and half of the night to bivouac near Pamplin's Station, on the South Side Railroad.

Sunday morning, April 9th, 1865, Lee made a last and desperate attempt to escape by cutting his way through the lines of the cavalry. We broke camp after only two hours rest, and after three hours of forced marching in the direction of brisk artillery firing, came up to the right and rear of the cavalry, who had been pressed back for some distance by Lee's attack. At the sight of the bayonets of our approaching corps the Confederates ceased their attempt, and withdrew to their lines of the morning.

It was the good fortune of the 32d Regiment to be that day at the head of the column. The day was fine but not uncomfortably warm; the men in the best of spirits, fully imbued with the feeling that the end was near. In this our last fight the conditions were unusually favorable for infantry movements, the country rolling but open, and covered with grassy turf.

A change of direction to the right brought us out of the road and into an open field of pasture-land which rose before us on a gentle slope for nearly half a mile. Entering this field, and without a halt, the Regiment formed column of companies, then formed divisions, and then deployed on the rear division. No battalion movement was ever executed more precisely or with lines better dressed. Waiting a moment for the other regiments of the brigade to complete their formation, we saw before us the swell of land on which we stood, and beyond, on higher ground, the enemy's artillery, with infantry supports, in line of battle. It was a glorious sight — the beauty of the spring morning — the gentle movement of the air — the rich garniture of green which everywhere clad the view — all were exhilarating, while the universal conviction that the enemy, now in full sight, was also within our power, inspired the men with such enthusiasm as made every man to feel himself invincible.

Soon came the order, "Forward." The colors never came more promptly to the front, and the right and left general guides fairly sprang to their positions. The enemy being in full sight no skirmishers preceded us. The advance was made under a sharp artillery fire, the men stepping out with a full thirty-six inch stride. The enemy's front line was slowly falling back. At the summit of the rising ground, where we received a few stray rifle shots, we could see that the ground fell off for perhaps six hundred yards, to where a little stream — one of the head waters of the Appomatox — ran winding along. Here, just as we expected to receive the volleys of the enemy, his firing suddenly ceased, and a halt was ordered.

Colonel Cunningham, through his field-glass, seeing what seemed to be a flag of truce in our front, took the adjutant with him, and, putting spurs to their horses, they dashed forward, and soon met a mounted officer attended by an orderly, bearing a small white flag upon a staff. This officer announced

himself as one of General Lee's staff, and said that
he was the bearer of a message to General Grant
with a view to surrender. The flag was duly
reported, and very soon an officer representing General Grant appeared, and the colonel and adjutant
retired.

Soon the expected surrender of Lee was known
through all our lines, and the hearts of all were
joyous and gay — perfectly so, except for a shade of
regret that we could not have finished a fight which
promised so well for us.

The two commanding generals met about eleven
o'clock in a small house a little way off to our right
and front. Our corps was in line by divisions
closed in mass, the orders being to keep the men
well in hand; but the general talk was that the war
was over, and that we should soon turn the heads of
our columns north.

At 2.30 P. M. we knew that the surrender was a
fact, and that it would be officially promulgated at 4
P. M.

Meantime was a season of general and heartfelt
mutual congratulations, during which it was noticed
that General Gregory's brigade was forming square,
off on the near hillside, and several officers of our
brigade mounted and rode over to see what was
going on.

Brigadier-General Gregory had a gift for prayer
and speech, and also a resonant voice. From the
centre of his square he made a rousing good speech
of congratulation, and then, calling to prayer, commenced a hearty thanksgiving to God for the success

which had attended our arms, and for the reasonable hope of an early return to peaceful homes.

Just then, miles away to our left, a detachment of General Fitz Hugh Lee's cavalry, having sighted a Union supply train — being very hungry and not knowing of the truce, pitched into the escort with artillery and carbines, and the boom, boom, boom of his guns smote upon the ear of Gregory. The general ceased abruptly, listened, and again boom, boom, boom came the sound well known to his practiced ear, and then again his voice rang out: " Never mind the rest, men — reduce square — form brigade line ;" and in three minutes all were ready for action.

The official order came at four o'clock, and after a pretty lively evening we were glad to be at rest in bivouac.

April 10th. — A very quiet, restful day ; the officers and men of the two armies making and returning visits. The officers of our Regiment, with others of the division, attended General Chamberlain in calls of courtesy upon General Lee and other officers of the surrendered forces. The Confederates were entirely out of rations and, although we were also short by reason of our rapid advance and the woful condition of the roads, our men readily assented to divide the contents of their haversacks with the soldiers who had so long been their enemy, and throughout the day the officers and men of the two armies were to be seen thoroughly commingled. Confederate States currency was to be had by the bushel.

April 11th was the day appointed for the formal surrender of the arms. General Chamberlain, commanding our division, was detailed in charge of the ceremony, and our brigade was ordered to receive the arms of the rebel infantry.

At 9 A. M. the brigade was formed in line on a road leading from our camp to that of the Confederates, its right in the direction of the latter. The 32d Massachusetts was the extreme right of the brigade. The Confederate troops came up by brigades at route step, arms-at-will. In some regiments the colors were rolled tightly to the staff, but in others the bearers flourished them defiantly as they marched. As they approached our line, our men stood at shouldered arms, the lines were carefully dressed, and eyes front; seeing which, and appreciating the compliment implied, some of the enemy's brigadiers closed up their ranks, and so moved along our front with their arms at the shoulder. Their files marched past until their right reached to our left, when they halted, fronted facing us, stacked their arms, hung their accoutrements upon the rifles, and then the colorbearer of each regiment laid his colors across the stacks, and the brigade, breaking to its rear, gave room for the next to come up in its place, and each successive brigade observed the same order of proceeding, upon the same ground.

As the first brigade moved away, a detail of our men took the stacks as they stood, and moved them up nearer to our line, and the arms from the stacks of each succeeding brigade were taken by the same detail and piled around the first stacks; so that when the ceremony was ended there was but one line of stacks, with the equipments and colors hanging or lying thereupon.

Throughout the whole our men behaved nobly — not only was there no cheering or exultation, but there was, on the contrary, a feeling of deep soldierly sympathy for their gallant enemy, which evinced itself in respectful silence, and this conduct was appreciated and warmly commended by many of the rebel officers.

It was 4 P. M. before the surrender was completed, and the rest of the day and evening was given up to jovial congratulations among ourselves.

After the surrender we were employed for some days in guarding the railroads and public property; and then started for Washington, which we reached by easy marches, and on the 12th of May pitched our last camp on Arlington Heights. With the Army of the Potomac we passed in review before the President, on the 22d of May, and on the 29th of June started for home. At Philadelphia and again at Providence we were refreshed by the hospitality of the citizens, and about noon of July 1st we arrived in Boston, marching directly to the Common, where the men were furloughed until the 6th.

On the 6th of July the command again assembled on Boston Common, and proceeded to Gallops Island, where, on the 11th July, 1865, it was paid off and mustered out of service, and the 32d Massachusetts Infantry was no more.

Only a narrow strip of water in the bay divides the two islands where were passed its first days and its last.

It was a noble battalion, one which won alike the compliments of its generals, and the confidence of its associate regiments. No officer's life was ever sacrificed because of any want of steadiness of the men, and more than once they executed tactical movements under fire, in a manner that would have been creditable if done on parade. During and since the war great *esprit du corps* has been characteristic of its soldiers. Many of them have attained to prominence in the walks of peaceful life, to the great rejoicing of their comrades, and many have made their final march. — God give them rest in peace.

The extreme length of service in the Regiment was three years, seven months, and twenty-five days.

The total number of officers commissioned in the Regiment was 75, of whom 34 were at one time or another reported among the casualties, namely:

Killed or mortally wounded, - - 5
Died of disease contracted in the service, 2
Wounded and returned to duty, - 17
Discharged for disability, - - - 10
         Total, - - - - —34

The total number of men enlisted was 2,286, of whom 520 were at some time non-commissioned officers, and 60 received commissions.

R

There were —
Killed in battle,   -   -   -   -   76
Died of wounds or disease, -   -   - 194
Discharged for disability,   -   -   384
                                                    ——

    Total loss to the Regiment by cas-
      ualties,   -   -   -   -   - 654

This total does not include the number of men wounded who returned to duty ; nor of those, some 200 more, who died in captivity or by the roadside in severe marches, who are included in the returns among the unaccounted for, missing, and deserters.

The number discharged at the expiration of their service was 1,087.

Of the 37 commissioned officers who were included in the final muster out of the Regiment, all except seven were promoted from the ranks.

ROSTER AT THE EXPIRATION OF SERVICE.

COLONEL:
J. CUSHING EDMUNDS, *Brevet Brig. General.*

LIEUTENANT COLONEL:
JAMES A. CUNNINGHAM, *Brevet Brig. General.*

MAJOR:
EDWARD O. SHEPARD, *Brevet Lieut. Colonel.*

ADJUTANT:
CAPTAIN ISAAC F. KINGSBURY.

SURGEON:
SAMUEL W. FLETCHER.

ASSISTANT SURGEON:
JOHN McGREGOR.

Co. A. *Captain*, John E. Tidd.
1st Lieut., Abner E. Drury.
2d Lieut.,

Co. B. *Captain*, Ambrose Bancroft, *Brevet Major.*
1st Lieut., Joseph P. Robinson.
2d Lieut., William F. Taft.

Co. C. *Captain*, Timothy McCartney, *Brevet Major.*
1st Lieut., George A. Batchelder.
2d Lieut., William F. Tuttle.

Co. D.   *Captain,*
1st Lieut., Loring Burrill, commanding Co.
2d Lieut., Charles N. Gardner.

Co. E.   *Captain,*
1st Lieut., Stephen C. Phinney, comd'g Co. `
2d Lieut.,

Co. F.   *Captain,* John A. Bowdlear.
1st Lieut., Asa L. Kneeland.
2d Lieut.,

Co. G.   *Captain,* George W. Lauriat, *Brevet Major.*
1st Lieut., Jos. S. Wyman, Capt. not must'd.
2d Lieut., Charles H. Bartlett.

Co. H.   *Captain,* William E. Reed.
1st Lieut., Augustus A. Coburn.
2d Lieut.,

Co. I.   *Captain,* Isaac W. Smith.
1st Lieut., James H. Clapp.
2d Lieut., James W. King.

Co. K.   *Captain,* George A. Hall.
1st Lieut., James P. Wade.
2d Lieut.,

Co. L.   *Captain,* James E. March.
1st Lieut., George H. Ackerman.
2d Lieut.,

Co. M.   *Captain,* Charles H. Smith.
1st Lieut., Thomas Coos.
2d Lieut., Lyndon Y. Jenness.

Unattached and not mustered:
2d Lieut., Dwight B. Graves.
2d Lieut., Charles E. Madden.
2d Lieut., Edward Knights.

2186-16

LaVergne, TN USA
26 January 2011
214002LV00009B/169/A